T0138641

Internet-Scale Pattern Recognition

New Techniques for Voluminous
Data Sets and Data Clouds

Internet-Scale Pattern Recognition

New Techniques for Voluminous Data Sets and Data Clouds

Anang Hudaya Muhamad Amin
Asad I. Khan
Benny B. Nasution

CRC Press
Taylor & Francis Group
Boca Raton   London   New York

CRC Press is an imprint of the
Taylor & Francis Group, an **informa** business

A CHAPMAN & HALL BOOK

CRC Press
Taylor & Francis Group
6000 Broken Sound Parkway NW, Suite 300
Boca Raton, FL 33487-2742

© 2013 by Taylor & Francis Group, LLC
CRC Press is an imprint of Taylor & Francis Group, an Informa business

No claim to original U.S. Government works

Printed and bound in Great Britain by TJ International, Padstow, Cornwall
Version Date: 2012924

International Standard Book Number: 978-1-4665-1096-8 (Hardback)

Library of Congress Cataloging-in-Publication Data

Muhamad Amin, Anang Hudaya.
    Internet-scale pattern recognition : new techniques for voluminous data sets and data clouds / Anang Hudaya Muhamad Amin, Asad Khan, Benny Nasution.
        p. cm.
    Includes bibliographical references and index.
    ISBN 978-1-4665-1096-8 (hardback)
    1. Data mining. 2. Pattern recognition systems. 3. Web usage mining. 4. Mathematical statistics--Data processing. I. Khan, Asad II. Nasution, Benny. III. Title.

QA76.9.D343M84 2012
006.3'12--dc23   2012031622

Visit the Taylor & Francis Web site at
http://www.taylorandfrancis.com

and the CRC Press Web site at
http://www.crcpress.com

"Knowledge is the conformity of the object and the intellect." — *Averroes*

Contents

III   Systems and Tools   91

IV   Implementations and Applications   107

Preface

We would argue that the thinking behind pattern recognition has been inordinately constrained by the characteristics of prevailing computing machinery. Otherwise, given the volume of literature on pattern recognition that has been generated over the past 50 years, it would be fair to expect that some elementary forms of human vision or hearing would be demonstrable by now. It is not feasible to model processes that take place in the human brain as stored programs on sequential processors. The technology in this regard tethers on edges. Reading text reliably only works in tightly controlled environments. Similarly, recognizing the simplest of spoken words cannot be guaranteed when the speech style is subtly altered. Recognizing other types of sounds remains a work in progress.

Pattern recognition, even at the simplest levels available to a newborn, remains beyond the grasp of contemporary algorithms. We need to question the fundamentals that have been driving research in this area for over half a century. Why is the level of pattern recognition available to the simplest of biological brains not yet achievable by computers? Is there an unknown factor, the absence of which is making it impossible to implement reliable pattern recognition? Are we missing something obvious? Without entering the realm of quantum mechanics, we will address these questions and put forth views that may seem somewhat unorthodox and challenge conventional wisdom. Maverick claims alone will certainly not prove the validity of our arguments. Therefore, we will methodically build up evidence by describing our techniques and putting forth the results. If we can demonstrate elementary forms of human pattern recognition on a machine, it is important that we also describe the applications that will make use of it.

With better computers and greater connectivity, we are rapidly approaching the limits of conventional technologies. Vast amounts of data are starting to appear, but there are no clear means to benefit from the data without substantial human intervention. With the exception of a few very narrow applications, there is very little scope for independent machine action. As computers generate more data and networks communicate at higher speeds, the human operator becomes the bottleneck. In the absence of reliable machine intelligence, the human operator must personally manage continuous streams of information. Let us consider the case of a highly skilled radiologist who can access the records of patients remotely. Sophisticated means to access patient data provide no relief to our lone specialist. However, this operator-level bottleneck can be alleviated if the preliminary reading of images can be entrusted to machines. In doing so, the machines must perform reliably under all unforeseeable variations in data and must be able to keep up with the data streams' reliability and speed. The main focus of the research presented in this text is to unveil a computational model that will supply performance and scalability to achieve higher levels of reliability. However, to truly grasp the essence of these techniques, one must exorcise some of the preconceived notions of machine intelligence, especially with respect to iterative learning in artificial neural networks.

The phrase "the network is the computer," attributed to John Gage when he was with Sun Microsystems, may have been a good slogan to capture the market exuberance of the late 1990s. However, this statement also carries profound technical meaning, especially if we add to it and re-state: the network is the "better" computer. Only a network can increase its size indefinitely under the proper conditions. Therefore, a network that computes may continue to increase its capacity without the bottleneck of the von Neumann archetype. Equally, if not more importantly, only the network pathways provide an endless source of parallelism. A computer that is embodied within a network will continue to increase its computational prowess and parallelism. It is important to distinguish between a logical network simulated as a stored computer program in the conventional archetype and a program that automatically distributes itself across every link of the network, i.e., an in-network program. It may be asked, if all that is needed is a new type of computer archetype and an accompanying programming style, why has it not yet been designed? The answer lies in the way knowledge disciplines are organized. To make this relatively simple concept a reality, strong interactions among the networking, parallel and distributed computing, and artificial intelligence disciplines are required. There are powerful disincentives to working across disciplines, and the collective volume of literature thwarts individual effort. Therefore, it is important that knowledge is extracted and suitably trimmed for the purpose at hand. This text draws upon concepts from pattern recognition, parallel processing, distributed systems, and data networks and presents the concise body of knowledge that is required for reliable and scalable pattern recognition.

Looking ahead, we see steady growth in devices other than the standard computers being attached to the Internet. Some of these devices carry sensors and are able to extensively read their surroundings. In particular, wireless sensor networks offer intriguing possibilities. Commodity devices, such as smart phones, also carry considerable environment-sensing hardware. The demand to recognize event signatures, perhaps even predict certain types of events, is inevitable once such devices become part of daily life. We expect that the knowledge presented in this text will help with the programming of large networks of devices and will provide an extendable template for Internet-scale pattern recognition applications.

Khan first published the key principles of programming a network to function as a scalable, single-cycle learning, associative memory system in 2002 [1]. Mihailescu and Khan [2] later found that the technique was vulnerable to the pattern crosstalk problem. Nasution and Khan [3] addressed this vulnerability by hierarchically connecting the networks, and the results were published in early 2008. The approach was vastly improved by Muhamad Amin and Khan [4] by introducing knowledge from the parallel and distributed computing domain into a solution derived from the integration of the data networking and artificial intelligence domains. Therefore, we hope that this text, which is based on our research efforts of the past 10 years, will shorten the learning curve for our readers and provide them with valuable insights for further innovation.

Acknowledgments

We hereby acknowledge the following people and organizations for their contributions to this book: Amir Basirat, Amiza Amir, Raja Azlina Raja Mahmood, and Professor Bala Srinivasan of Clayton School of Information Technology, Monash University, Australia, for their constructive critique and helpful ideas in building the contents of this book. Fredrik Sandin, Blerim Emruli, Sven Molin and other people from EISLAB, Luleå Technical University, Sweden for their comments and other contributions, as part of the STINT (Swedish Foundation for International Cooperation in Research and Higher Education) collaborative research project. We are also grateful for the continuous support and help from the publishing team at CRC Press, including Li-Ming Leong and Randi Cohen. Finally, to all our family, colleagues and friends who have endlessly supported us in many different ways, ensuring the success of this book.

About the Authors

Anang Hudaya Muhamad Amin, PhD, is a senior lecturer in the Faculty of Information Science and Technology, Multimedia University, Malaysia. He received a BTech (Hons.) in Information Technology from Universiti Teknologi PETRONAS, Malaysia, and Master of Network Computing and PhD from Monash University, Australia. His research interests include artificial intelligence with specialization in distributed pattern recognition and bio-inspired computational intelligence, wireless sensor networks, and distributed computing.

Asad I. Khan, PhD, received his BSc from the University of Engineering and Technology, Lahore, Pakistan in 1980. He received the MSc with distinction from Heriot-Watt University, Edinburgh, UK in 1990, and was awarded a PhD in 1994 by the Faculty of Engineering at Heriot-Watt University. He was appointed a lecturer at Heriot-Watt in 1993 and later took up a computer centre management role at Monash University in Australia. During this period he was involved with the design of large storage and high performance computing projects. He was appointed a senior lecturer in the Faculty of Information Technology at Monash University in 2000. During this period he co-authored one of the first books on parallel finite element computations. Dr. Khan's work on parallel processing, evolutionary computing, and bio-inspired techniques has led to several large research grants from British, Australian, and Swedish Research Councils and leading industrial bodies. He is a co-recipient of two large research grants from the Australian government. His theoretical research areas comprise parallel computation, neural networks, and distributed pattern recognition. His applied research involves development of e-research systems and intelligent sensor networks. He is an Australian Research Council assessor and regularly reviews for a number of leading computing and engineering publication outlets. His research has been reported in leading newspapers and online media such *The Age, Sydney Morning Herald, Computer World, ZD-NET*, and *Research News*. He has been invited to speak at the University of Melbourne, Australia; University of Coimbra, Portugal; NATO Advance Research Workshop, Sesimbra, Portugal; and the NATO Advance Study Institute, Berchestgaden, Germany. He has published over 80 fully refereed papers.

Benny B. Nasution, PhD, received a Dipl.Ing. from Switzerland in 1993, then a MEng and PhD from Australia in 2000 and 2007, respectively. He was awarded a Swiss Government Scholarship for 1989–1995, and an Australian Government Scholarship from 1998 to 2000 and 2002 to 2007. In 2004, he was awarded the IBM Award at Tokyo Research Lab (TRL) in Japan. In 2007 he won the Mollie Holman Medal (the best thesis of the year).

Part I

Recognition: A New Perspective

Chapter 1

Introduction

"One is obliged to admit that perception and what depends upon it is inexplicable on mechanical principles, that is, by figures and motions. In imagining that there is a machine whose construction would enable it to think, to sense, and to have perception, one could conceive it enlarged while retaining the same proportions, so that one could enter into it, just like into a windmill. Supposing this, one should, when visiting within it, find only parts pushing one another, and never anything by which to explain a perception."
— **Leibniz**, *Monadology*

1.1   As We See, We Learn

As human beings, our physiological structure enables us to look, speak, hear, taste, smell, touch, and feel our surroundings. If we look at a familiar object, say a tree, we can tell that it is a tree and not a chimney or a water reservoir. Our ability to recognize and differentiate between objects that we see, hear, and touch would not be possible without the presence of a powerful sensory system. Our brain and our nervous system allow us to experience our surroundings through a combination of senses and memories.

It is estimated that the human brain comprises approximately 80 to 120 billion neurons, which respond to a multitude of actions, perceptions, and emotions. From a physical perspective, our brains could be considered as large-scale interconnected networks of sensory systems and memories. Seeing, identifying, and recalling what we have observed make up a significant portion of the activities conducted within these large-scale networks.

The recall process, also known as recognition, is a part of information processing that happens in our brain-nervous systems. Watkins and Gardiner [5] suggested a two-stage theory, in which recall begins with a search and retrieval process that is followed by a decision or recognition process. The correct information is chosen in the decision process from that which has been retrieved. Recognition of objects and other forms of events or stimuli is part of our brains' activities. Strong interest in this area has led to further understanding of the recognition process and how it can be performed using computational approaches. The study of the recognition process based on computational theories and the biological behavior of the nervous system can be traced back to the 1950s, when digital computers started being used for information processing. The ability to recognize and extract valuable information from raw data has motivated extensive research on pattern recognition techniques. Such techniques aspire to emulate the behavior of neural systems in living organisms.

To fully understand the concept of pattern recognition, there is a need to differentiate between some of the terms that are commonly used interchangeably, namely pattern recognition, data mining, and pattern classification.

Pattern recognition is the process of identifying an object or entity based on its descriptions and a set of measurements, commonly referred to as a pattern. Keeping with the previous example, a tree can be characterized by its vertical cylindrical shape, leaves, bark, and branches. In pattern recognition, we use these features to identify and differentiate a tree from other objects, such as a chimney or water reservoir.

To obtain useful information from data, it is important for applications to extract features or patterns. Pattern extraction from data is commonly known as data mining and involves uncovering patterns, associations, anomalies, interesting data structures, and traces of events. Recognition of patterns plays an important role in data mining applications in a variety of fields, including the life and physical sciences, economics, finance, and engineering.

Pattern classification is the process of assigning an object or entity to a class that shares similar characteristics or features. For example, biological taxonomy uses pattern classification to identify and label individuals as a class of species that have similar characteristics and behaviors.

The aim of any pattern recognition scheme is to achieve high recall accuracy for any recognition problem. However, almost every approach has to substantially increase its algorithmic complexity to accommodate this goal. Some promising approaches in assimilating and comprehending the functionalities of biological nervous systems have been proposed. Nevertheless, the highly cohesive procedures and processing-centric algorithmic design of these approaches may limit the capabilities of such approaches. Because requirements for the intensive collection and retrieval of data are appearing as a consequence of the data deluge phenomenon, it is important that we also consider the recognition process from the perspective of scalability.

1.2   Recognition at a Large Scale

Provided that we have solved the scalability problem, the Internet provides levels of connectivity and complexity that bear a resemblance to the human brain. Harnessing the potential of this interconnectivity of high-performance machines over large-scale networks may provide recognition schemes for large-scale and complex data. With the advent of high-resolution digital instruments and sensors in areas such as biomedical and satellite imaging, such large-scale and complex data are becoming increasingly available.

Machine intelligence is important in large-scale data applications. In biomedical imaging, intelligence schemes are commonly used to analyze and extract important and critical features from high-dimensional images obtained through sophisticated imaging techniques, such as Magnetic Resonance Imaging (MRI). In addition, computational intelligence schemes can be used by medical experts to assist in their diagnosis. With the advancements in high-speed networking technology, medical experts can conduct a collaborative diagnosis by collecting data from instruments over large networks and storing or updating these data in distributed repositories. With this capability at hand, the amount of data generated as part of the distributed system is at the Internet-scale.

Depending on the in-depth resolution of satellite imaging, the size of the generated data can be huge. Satellite imaging is important in a number of applications, including the geographical information system (GIS) and the global positioning system (GPS). To produce useful geographical images, the raw images taken from the satellite camera must be processed. A number of processes are required, including image extraction and manipulation. These processes ensure that the data satisfy the resolution and size requirements for specific applications. Machine intelligence schemes can be very useful in performing these operations effectively.

A rapid growth in large-scale scientific analysis activities has inspired the development of sophisticated and state-of-the-art facilities. One example is a synchrotron, a scientific facility that performs cyclic particle acceleration. The data generated by such facilities are images of the interaction of the particle beam with targets at a sub-atomic scale. An average beam line can produce hundreds of megabytes (Mb) of images continuously throughout the year. Synchrotron facilities are being used for a number of applications including large molecule crystallography and other chemical analyses. In addition, sophisticated data-capture instruments and sensors developed for high energy physics facilities, such as the Large Hadron Collider (see Figure 1.1) and Interferometric Synthetic Aperture Radar (InSAR), consistently generate extremely large volumes of highly complex and often invaluable data.

These state-of-the-art data capture and storage technologies are the key factors that have led to the generation of highly complex and large-scale data. The volumes alone make it impractical for data analysts to analyze and explore the data without the assistance of highly sophisticated computational tools. As mentioned earlier, the data mining and analysis capabilities of existing applications have not achieved their fullest potential. This shortfall is attributed mainly to the algorithmic complexity of existing data mining applications. For instance, the complexity of a decision tree classification tool

FIGURE 1.1: Inside the Large Hadron Collider (LHC) tunnel. An example of a large-scale data generation facility (Source: CERN).

can range from $O\left(n \log n\right)$ to $O\left(n^2\right)$ or worse, depending on the type of pruning applied [6]. These types of algorithms are computationally expensive and infeasible for large data sets.

The integration of computational devices within the Internet architecture has seen rapid expansion in commodity use items, such as phones, and commodity use infrastructures, such as roads. Sensory data are generated and used remotely to interact with the environment. This connectivity between devices and sensory-enabled objects is commonly known as the Internet-of-Things (IoT) and proposes pervasive computability and sensor-led control through a plethora of smart objects, around us. These smart objects are everyday physical things that have been enhanced with a small electronic device to provide local intelligence and connectivity to the Internet [7]. This enhancement bridges the gap between the physical and information domains. With seamless connectivity between smart objects and high-performance computational systems, such as Internet servers, it may become possible for us to create large-scale sense-compute systems that exhibit the efficiencies of biological nervous systems.

Imagine a household equipped with fully connected smart devices with embedded sensors. These sensors would detect the level of heat emitted by each attached device and collectively determine the heat level generated. Information on current weather conditions obtained from the Internet could then be used to adjust the thermostat of an air-conditioner to load-balance the heat from all of the devices with the existing room/house conditions, thus creating an intelligent and adaptive heat control system. To be effective, this sensing capability requires a massive amount of data to be extracted continuously in real-time. Therefore, a mechanism to extract these data should be considered. In this context, we can use patterns to represent a collection of sensory data over a specific timeframe. We can implement recognition on these patterns to detect and adjust the level of heat required.

As another example, one can imagine wirelessly connected sensors embedded along a road between two cities, primarily for the purpose of traffic management. The sensors could signal an incoming tsunami or seismic event and provide invaluable minutes before a cataclysmic event. Such a network could also provide real-time data for calculating routes and arrival times.

An environment where sensors are embedded in smart objects and living infrastructures, such as roads and buildings, provides seamless monitoring of our living conditions and more effective means of conducting our day-to-day activities. Consider the use of sensor networks that are attached to roads for traffic monitoring. In a peak period when many vehicles pass a particular intersection with traffic lights, the sensors will communicate with the traffic light system to change the system settings to allow more vehicles to pass through on a congested route. Indirectly, such systems will improve the quality of life for people.

The state of miniaturization and cost of production of wireless sensors make it quite feasible to build such systems. However, one major impediment prevents their implementation. The data arising from the sensors would be incessant, and due to the rapid generation of sensory data from the nodes, the data will rapidly become extremely large. Therefore, any such system must continue to keep up with data using superior filtering, storage, and processing.

To fully understand the information gained from these sensor data, a mechanism to learn and adapt to its characteristics is required. The sensor data that fit into the spatial and/or temporal domains would generate a signature and/or trend for a given space and/or time. This signature can be detected using a pattern recognition approach.

The data deluge phenomenon that we are currently experiencing is affecting the way that we process these data. It is not realistic to use simple analytical means to understand the information obtained from a multitude of sources with large magnitudes of size and dimension. A paradigm shift in data processing is necessary. Common pattern recognition applications that execute within a CPU-centric environment to recall or memorize megabytes or gigabytes of data may not be effective when processing terabytes of data. The recognition scheme must be considered from a larger perspective, i.e., the Internet-scale perspective.

pattern recognition is a term that will be referred to as recognition involving large-scale data. These data may be coming from different sources ranging from sophisticated devices and facilities to simple but large-scale data collection mechanisms, such as a wireless sensor network (WSN) deployment for monitoring environmental conditions. The key aspect of Internet-scale pattern recognition is a larger capacity for the recognition of data. Therefore, the means by which data are analyzed must scale with the growth of the data. There are several key technologies that contribute to this Internet-scale pattern recognition approach. These include distributed systems, parallel computing technologies, and machine intelligence. In its simplest definition, a distributed system is a collection of independent computers that appear to be a single coherent system to its users. Formally, a distributed system is a computer architecture containing multiple inter-connected processors. These processors are inter-connected via communication networks that perform a particular task or operate collectively.

A distributed system offers resource-sharing capabilities and is able to adapt to the incremental growth of resources. It also provides reliable resource availability. Distributed systems have evolved from topological networks, such as the Ethernet, to the current cloud computing technology. Cloud computing is a form of utility computing that enables large-scale activities and operations to be performed beyond the boundaries of local networks or within a particular organizational structure. The large amount of resources available within the computational cloud provides the means for performing complex large-scale engineering or scientific analyses, including recognizing data at the Internet-scale.

Parallel computing technology addresses how information can be processed more efficiently. Our universe can be viewed as a parallel computer, in which all of the elements perform their operations simultaneously. In the last several decades, parallel computing technology has advanced from simple multi-threading computations to multi-core and graphical processing unit (GPU) computing technologies. By performing concurrent computations, parallel computing enables large-scale problems to be solved more efficiently. For extensive pattern recognition processes on existing Internet-scale data, parallel computing is a similar to the discovery of fire.

The rapid development of machine intelligence schemes is also contributing to the development of Internet-scale pattern recognition. From classical statistical approaches to sophisticated machine learning techniques, computational intelligence schemes are critically important in numerical analysis and other experimentations involving scientific data. Nevertheless, a key issue that needs to be addressed is the scalability of such schemes when processing Internet-scale data.

This book describes fundamental research on the scalability of pattern recognition. Scalability in the context of pattern recognition can be defined as the ability to either handle growing amounts of patterns in a graceful manner or to be readily enlarged. The scalability issues of the existing pattern recognition schemes for Internet-scale data deployment will be presented. A number of different approaches will be extensively reviewed, and a number of possible solutions for the scalability problem will be introduced.

1.3 Computational Intelligence Approach for Pattern Recognition

The development of computational intelligence schemes can be traced back to the first computational intelligence test conducted by Alan Turing in 1950. Computational intelligence involves schemes that use a set of procedures and operations to mimic the intelligence of biological organisms. One of the best examples is the biological neural system that has been implemented by the artificial neural network (ANN) approach.

The artificial neural network (ANN) approach was defined in the 1950s by the introduction of the Perceptron approach by Rosenblatt [8]. The concept of an artificial neural network is fundamental to neural computing, which emerged from the knowledge and understanding of how biological neural systems store and manipulate information. Neural networks can be considered as massive parallel computing systems comprising a large number of small, interconnected processors, known as neurons [9]. One of the benefits of ANN-based pattern recognition is that it allows the system to learn and adapt to the nature of the data. This adaptive feature allows the recognition schemes to be used in a wide range of applications. Therefore, it may offer a more scalable approach for large-scale recognition. Figure 1.2 shows a generic example of a neural network structure for pattern recognition.

Pattern recognition applications that use the neural network approach rely heavily on the learning algorithm. This algorithm is essential to determine the efficiency and accuracy of the pattern store and recall operations. Learning algorithms use a sequential training procedure to allow neural networks to learn complex non-linear input-output relationships and adapt themselves to the data. Prominent approaches in learning algorithms include Hebbian learning [10] and incremental learning [11].

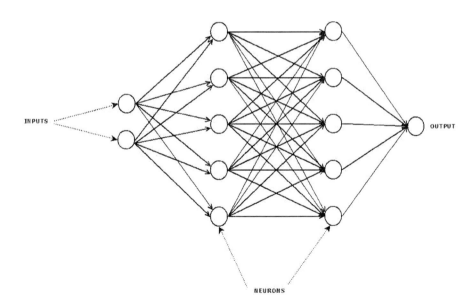

FIGURE 1.2: Generic neural network architecture for pattern recognition with two layers of hidden neurons.

Apart from neural networks, machine learning is also widely used in pattern recognition. Machine learning, as defined by Nilsson [12] refers to changes in the systems that perform tasks associated with artificial intelligence (AI). Machine learning is also considered to be a deterministic approach for pattern recognition. It is commonly used in conjunction with other neural network schemes. Some examples of machine learning approaches include genetic programming, support vector machines (SVMs), and Bayesian networks.

Implementations of machine learning approaches for pattern recognition require *a priori* knowledge of the types of functions or kernel machines to be used for a specific recognition domain. For instance, a linear SVM has the ability to perform classification on binary problems and is not suitable for multi-class domains. For the machine to work on a specific set of data, the machine learning approach commonly requires extensive and iterative learning procedures to obtain the best parameter estimates. These two issues affect the feasibility of using the machine learning approach to design a scalable and generic pattern recognition scheme.

Machine learning approaches based on ANNs offer low levels of both scalability and adaptability, which are mainly due to the following criteria of neural network approaches:

1. Some neural network/machine learning approaches can be conducted within a parallel environment, e.g., Hopfield networks and feed-forward neural networks. This parallelization capability enables recognition to be conducted on large-scale data. However, the complexity of these algorithms hinders its capability to perform pattern recognition in a purely parallel manner.

2. Enhancements in unsupervised machine learning schemes, such as the K-mean clustering algorithm, provide an opportunity for heterogeneous patterns and data to be used in the recognition processes. Nevertheless, these algorithms require strenuous training and complex recognition procedures.

3. Limited storage capacity. For example, to obtain optimum recognition, the number of estimated random patterns stored by the Hopfield network is $0.138N$ where N represents the number of units in the network [13].

4. Some neural networks can learn from the data used in the recognition process. However, memorization by the learning process requires a large number of similar class data.

In addition, ANNs and other machine learning approaches suffer from a number of issues, including the following:

1. For many neural network schemes, the iterative procedure in the weight adjustment during data training, such as the feed-forward network, imposes significant delays in processing.

2. Over-fitting problem: A small training set cannot represent actual large-scale data.

3. The recognition function within neural networks or machine learning works only for a specific problem within the recognition domain. Network retraining is required for different sets of problems.

The existing literature on computational intelligence shows that the scalability and adaptability of machine learning approaches outweigh other pattern recognition approaches. Some machine learning approaches can be used in parallel environments, and recognition loads are distributed across computational nodes. Nevertheless, these algorithms require extensive and complex computations to derive the best solution for the recognition process.

1.4 Scalability in Pattern Recognition

The emergence of the data deluge phenomenon has brought forward the need for recognition schemes for Internet-scale patterns. We can divide large-scale pattern recognition into two perspectives. The first perspective is recognition of a large number of patterns. In this context, the focus is on the volume of the patterns. The recognition process recognizes or classifies patterns into a large number of clusters, and a large number of patterns are stored. The second perspective is recognition of large patterns. In this case, the pattern data are huge, as in the areas of face or image recognition.

In this section, we consider some of the common barriers encountered when implementing pattern recognition for large-scale data sets and some of the possible solutions. Our interest lies in the implementation of widely available distributed computing infrastructures for scalable pattern recognition schemes.

1.4.1 Common Barriers

Pattern recognition is an important tool in evaluating and analyzing large-scale data that have been produced in a wide range of applications. Nevertheless, current approaches incur excessive computational complexity to adapt to these large and highly complex data sets. When processing large and highly complex data sets, there are a number of barriers that need to be addressed with respect to the implementation of pattern recognition. These include the following:

1. *Size of data:* As the size of the data set increases, existing pattern recognition schemes must be able to manage data in an efficient manner with specific concerns for storage and transport. Methods in a recognition

process that store and communicate data must take into account the size of the data sets used.

2. *Dimensions of data:* The sophisticated approaches in data capture technology allow for highly dimensional data to be extracted from the environment. In this context, pattern recognition applications must be able to cater to different dimensionalities of data in their implementations.

3. *Algorithmic complexity:* Existing pattern recognition schemes are powerful and have the ability to provide highly accurate solutions. Nevertheless, they incur high algorithmic complexity in their implementations, which is attributed to the iterative nature and complex mathematical foundations of the algorithms. Some algorithms are exponential and infeasible for large-scale data. Furthermore, the expensive computations of existing pattern recognition schemes can be computationally time-consuming, especially when processing complex large-scale data.

These barriers are the common factors in determining the scalability of a particular pattern recognition approach. Each approach must be able to address increasing size and dimensionality of the data, while minimizing its complexity. In this regard, scalability evaluations of existing pattern recognition schemes are valuable to most pattern recognition application developers.

1.4.2   Possible Solutions

Scalability is an important factor in today's pattern recognition approaches. The existing outgrowth of data in daily usage shows that the capability of existing algorithms must continue to grow to serve these Internet-scale data. For example, according to Anderson [14], every 72 minutes there is one petabyte of data processed by Google's server. This value will continue to increase as the storage and processing mechanisms advance. The question of scalability as described by Pal and Mitra [15] is as follows: Can the pattern recognition algorithm process large data sets efficiently, while building from them the best possible models?

There are several techniques to scale up pattern recognition algorithms for large-scale data sets. These techniques can be divided into a number of approaches:

1. *Data Approach:* This type of technique modifies the data prior to the recognition process. Some of the techniques are data reduction, dimensionality reduction, and data partitioning. The aim of this approach is to minimize the size and dimensionality of the data for efficient recognition. However, this approach may undermine the data integrity by representing the large data domain using a small data set.

2. *Learning Approach:* Pattern recognition algorithms require a learning mechanism. This mechanism may be computationally expensive. There-

fore, reducing the complexity of the learning mechanism is an objective of scalability. Examples of improving scalability using the learning approach include active learning [16] and incremental learning [11]. A significant limitation of this approach is that the accuracy of the algorithm may be sacrificed for the sake of fast and simple learning capabilities.

3. *Distributed Computing Approach:* The advancement in networking technologies has enabled large-scale computations to be performed within the body of a network itself. Rapid developments in high performance computing and grid technologies allow a collaboration of resources to work for a specific application. In this context, existing pattern recognition algorithms may be implemented on a distributed computing platform using parallel processing. Some examples of scalable pattern recognition schemes using this approach include the works carried out in [1, 17].

1.4.3 Distributed Computing Solution for Scalability of PR Schemes

The distributed computing approach for scaling existing pattern recognition algorithms has the potential to be the optimum solution. However, some of the existing algorithms are highly complex and difficult to parallelize. Developments of neural network algorithms for pattern recognition have provided an interesting insight into the implementation of pattern recognition in distributed computing. In their nature, neural networks are formed through the collaboration of computational nodes, known as neurons. Due to the tightly coupled nature of existing neural network schemes, the integration of these two components is still in its infancy. It was initially conceived for single-processing (CPU-centric) architectures, which rely heavily on iterative techniques. Therefore, more work is needed to attain the effectiveness and efficiency of neural network algorithms for pattern recognition using the distributed computing approach.

Given the rapid advancement in existing distributed processing technologies, distributed computing may provide seemingly unlimited scalability for large-scale processing. Implementations of pattern recognition schemes in a distributed manner are possible in a variety of distributed computing environments using a simple, computationally inexpensive, and embarrassingly parallel recognition algorithm. Therefore, distributed pattern recognition (DPR) may be a solution for Internet-scale pattern recognition. Further discussions on the distributed computing approach will be presented in Chapter 2.

Chapter 2

Distributed Approach for Pattern Recognition

Implementing pattern recognition in a distributed manner may be a solution for the Internet-scale data generation and application problems. Distributed pattern recognition (DPR), the formal term for this type of recognition approach, can be defined as the extension of existing pattern recognition schemes to include the delegation of the recognition process across a distributed system. Most of the past initiatives in DPR have focused on providing a distributed architecture for pattern recognition [18, 19, 20, 21, 22]. However, this type of solution creates a high dependency on the hardware implementation. Because the implementation of these approaches across different architectural platforms and network environments is limited by their inflexibility, the issue of scalability in this context has yet to be solved.

A DPR scheme that is based solely on an algorithmic approach, independent of any hardware implementation, has yet to be fully realized. Though there are some recent studies on the implementation of a distributed approach for existing pattern recognition schemes [2, 23, 24, 25], these studies manipulated the methods of a particular algorithm to perform the recognition function (from sequential to parallel mechanisms). Furthermore, existing distributed approaches have been unable to reduce the computational complexity of their respective algorithms, a necessity for deployment in a distributed environment. In addition, these studies have not considered the communication costs incurred by the highly iterative features of the existing pattern recognition schemes.

The deployment of pattern recognition applications for large-scale data sets is an open issue that needs to be addressed. Several approaches have been proposed, including data reduction, active learning and distributed approaches in large-scale recognition. Nevertheless, a common denominator of these techniques is the algorithmic complexity of the recognition schemes. Because the distributed approach for pattern recognition can provide extensive support for resource availability in response to the increasing size, complexity and amount of data, it offers a significant advantage for large-scale data analysis. The ultimate goal for any DPR approach is to be able to extract useful information from a large-scale analysis of a huge collection of data.

Because pattern recognition is considered to be highly problem specific and has little prospect as a generic commodity application, DPR remains a relatively unexplored area. The complexity of existing pattern recognition algorithms limits their distribution factor. Several initiatives have attempted to parallelize and distribute a pattern recognition algorithm across a distributed system. However, the parallelization process poses a significant hurdle for this type of implementation.

The neural network approach is a promising tool for Internet-scale pattern recognition. This method has the ability to perform parallel computations using interconnected neurons. However, there are several implementation issues, including convergence problems, complex iterative learning procedures, and the fact that the training data required for optimum recognition leads to low scalability.

In this chapter, we will further discuss the important characteristics and aspects of DPR.

2.1   Scalability of Neural Network Approaches

In general, scalability can be achieved using a distributed approach. Therefore, the scalability factors for the pattern recognition schemes can be derived from the scalability requirements for any distributed system. There are two important factors that are closely related to the scalability of recognition schemes: storage capacity and inter-neuron communication frequency for neural network implementation. As Srinivas and Janakiram [26] explained, these two factors have been proposed based on the scalability requirements for distributed systems. The following subsections discuss these two factors in the context of common neural network approaches.

2.1.1   Pattern Storage Capacity

A baseline evaluation of storage capacity is based on how an increase in the number of stored patterns affects a given network. For each processing node, the memory capacity for pattern storage is analyzed. In recognition approaches, the importance of memory capacity lies in its ability to provide a scalable storage medium for large-scale patterns. Within a given neural network, the effect that the quantity of patterns has on the size of the memory required per node is evaluated.

Existing neural networks, such as Hopfield networks [27] (See Figure 2.1) and feed-forward neural networks, rely largely on the weight calculations in their recognition processes. In this context, each processing node would have a collection of weight-input values stored within its memory. For P patterns, the simplest approximation for the size of the memory, M, is given by the following equation:

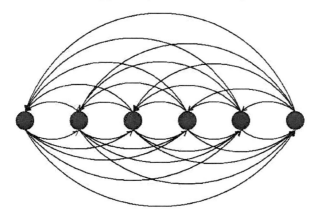

FIGURE 2.1: Hopfield neural network representation.

$$M = \sum_{n=1}^{P} w_n i_n \tag{2.1}$$

Where w represents the correlated weight, and i represents the input value for the nth stored pattern. This type of memory consumption effect occurs in different neural network schemes, including the feed-forward neural network, Hopfield network, radial basis function (RBF) neural network, morphological associative memory (MAM) [28], and Hamming associative memory [29]. The accuracy of the Hopfield network will significantly deteriorate if the number of patterns stored is greater than $0.138N$, where N represents the number of nodes in the network.

Not all neural network approaches have this type of memory representation. For instance, the memory representation of a Kohonen SOM [30] is different from other neural networks (See Figure 2.2). For each node in the SOM lattice, a pattern is represented using a vector-weight representation. Each node stores a set of weights for a particular pattern vector. Thus, for a d dimensional pattern vector, there is an equivalent number of weights, w; $w = d$.

2.1.2 Inter-Neuron Communication Frequency

The communication frequency of a neural network implementation is related to the number of communications, i.e., messages or signals, projected by a single node (or neuron) toward other nodes in the network. In actual implementations, a high communication frequency leads to network congestion, which limits the scalability of the recognition implementation. Therefore, for a network to be scalable, it is important that the communication frequency be kept to a minimum.

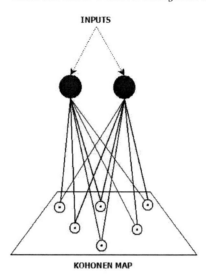

FIGURE 2.2: A Kohonen SOM node formation for a two-dimensional representation.

Communications between nodes in existing neural networks, such as feedforward, Hopfield, and RBF neural networks, are highly iterative in nature, which is due to the common weight adjustment/feedback methods used to generate an optimum result during recognition processes for a single pattern/pattern vector. Within multi-layer networks, the communication frequency of each node depends on the number of nodes per layer. For each pattern, the number of messages/signals communicated, C, by each node in a multi-layer network with n nodes per layer can be determined using the following equation:

$$C = nw \tag{2.2}$$

Where w is the number of iterations required for the weight adjustment. An increase in the size of the network or the number of weight adjustment iterations leads to a higher number of projected signals. Therefore, this approach is not an efficient scalable scheme for pattern recognition. Figure 2.3 illustrates this phenomenon.

A one-shot learning procedure is offered by some of the associative memory (AM) schemes for pattern recognition, including morphological and Hamming associative memories. This type of procedure reduces the need for an iterative process to derive optimum recognition results. Furthermore, this type of neural network performs lattice-based operations, in which communications between nodes are kept to a minimum, and operations are performed in a singular

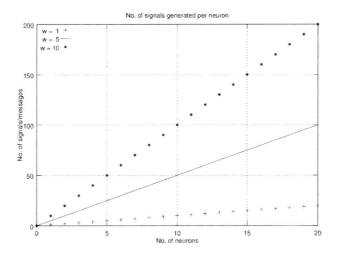

FIGURE 2.3: Estimated number of signals/messages generated, C by each neuron within a single layer of a common neural network scheme for several numbers of iterations, w.

manner, i.e., no collaboration between nodes. This effect of iterative procedure reduction is also experienced within a Kohonen SOM network.

The inability of most existing neural network schemes to scale up stems from their complex nature and iterative learning procedures. Furthermore, the training-validation-test mechanism produces significant delays in execution and creates a strong dependency between the training and test data. Therefore, there is a need to consider an algorithm that has limited complexity and training-test data dependency.

Although the scalability of a number of the existing neutral network schemes is limited, some intelligent recognition schemes are able to scale up with large-scale data, e.g., the one-shot learning Graph Neuron (GN) algorithm. The Graph Neuron (GN) is a graph-based associative memory algorithm [2, 31, 32] that is highly scalable and implements single-cycle learning for pattern recognition. Furthermore, the GN adopts an in-network processing approach, i.e., computational processes occur within the body of the network itself. The GN has been proposed for several pattern recognition implementations [33, 34].

2.2   Key Components of DPR

There are three main components of a scalable distributed pattern recognition scheme: the learning algorithms, the processing approach, and the training procedure.

2.2.1   Learning Mechanism

In pattern recognition, learning approaches play an important role in determining the efficiency and accuracy of the pattern store and recall operations. Prominent approaches include Hebbian learning [10], incremental learning [11], and one-shot learning. Hebbian learning is a classical learning technique that is based on the synaptic plasticity concept. The output of a neuron has a significant impact on the input to other neurons. Hebbian learning is a well-known technique for spatio-temporal pattern recognition in auto-associative neural networks. However, the potential for saturation and *"catastrophic forgetting"* makes the Hebbian learning technique less scalable. Most of the existing neural network algorithms implement Hebbian learning, including the Hopfield and feed-forward neural networks. A simple form of Hebbian learning follows the rule:

$$w_{ab} = x_a x_b \tag{2.3}$$

Where w_{ab} represents the weight connecting neuron b to a. The input of neuron a and postsynaptic response of neuron b are represented by x_a and x_b, respectively.

Incremental learning was developed to solve the scalability issue in pattern recognition [35]. It simplifies the problem of large training sets, specifically in machine learning algorithms, such as the Support Vector Machine (SVM) [36]. In incremental learning, training data are divided into several subsets. Each data subset individually undergoes a training phase. Subsequently, the results from each training session are combined to form the actual results. When there are a large number of training patterns, this training approach increases the scalability of the algorithm. However, problems are encountered when using the method to treat large-scale patterns. More computational resources are required to process larger patterns. Furthermore, this approach tends to be tightly coupled and requires computations of kernel functions, which are costly.

In one-shot learning, a minimal amount of initial data are required for a system to learn information. Past implementations of this learning mechanism used a probabilistic approach, such as the Bayesian classifier [37, 38]. Categories of objects can be learned from a small data set. One-shot learning will learn from the information obtained from these categories. In the sense that the learning process continues by the introduction of new patterns, the one-shot learning approach emulates incremental learning. The Graph Neuron (GN) [2] approach implements one-shot learning from a conceptually different perspective. The learning algorithm of a GN is implemented using the neuron-adjacency comparison approach.

2.2.2 Processing Approach

Distributing the input space within a pattern recognition algorithm improves the processing speed. Current trends in recognition approaches indicate a move toward parallel processing, in which recognition processes are carried out in parallel for different data sets.

Existing neural network recognition schemes, including Hopfield networks, are iterative in nature, and thus are time and resource intensive. These factors limit the ability of the existing recognition schemes to scale up as the quantity and size of the patterns stored increases. Furthermore, existing schemes are tightly coupled and have been developed only for single-processor environments. Numerous analyses have proven that parallel processing speeds-up the execution of processes. This follows Amdahl's law: when a higher fraction of the tasks can be parallelized, parallel processing can achieve the maximum speed. Figure 2.4 shows the estimated increase in speed (speedup) for processes containing different parallelizable portions. Note that as the fraction of the tasks that can be parallelized increases, the speed of the processes increases.

Parallel and distributed processing provides a fast processing mechanism that outperforms the single-processing approach. Nevertheless, in pattern recognition, the nature of the recognition algorithm makes it difficult to obtain an encompassing parallel approach.

2.2.3 Training Procedure

In the recognition context, training is the process of building up the algorithm for the actual recognition process. It allows the algorithm to learn from a sample data set before the actual recognition takes place. Depending on the requirements of the recognition algorithm, training can be achieved from small or large training data sets. In addition, training can be performed in a multi-cycle or single-cycle manner.

For generalization purposes, existing deterministic pattern recognition algorithms usually require large training data sets. In this view, the training data set should have all of the characteristics of the actual data. However, this is not usually the case. Furthermore, the nature of the learning mechanisms discussed earlier involve multi-cycle training.

Single-cycle training in learning was introduced by Khan [1] in the Graph Neuron (GN) implementation. The GN learning method involves recognizing adjacency values between neurons rather than revising weights between nodes,

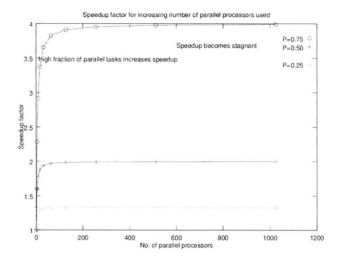

FIGURE 2.4: Comparison of the estimated processing speedup between recognition processes with different parallel fractions *(P)* as a function of the number of parallel processors used.

as in the Hebbian and incremental learning approaches. Because the training in a GN is conducted within a single-cycle, the recognition process is faster.

2.3   System Approaches

Existing distributed pattern recognition schemes have been designed and deployed using a top-down approach. Relatively CPU-centric (or sequential-based) algorithms were modified and enhanced to perform in a distributed manner. Furthermore, existing schemes tend to only partially apply the distribution mechanism, i.e., only in the context of training and validation. Some of these examples include feed-forward neural networks and self-organizing maps. Different types of distribution approaches have been considered [39]:

1. *Process Farming:* In this approach, the recognition process is distributed across a number of parallel processors. Each processor uses a copy of the algorithm to carry out a training process, as shown in Figure 2.5. In this configuration, each processing network consists of a master node and several worker nodes. Each worker node performs training or recognition processes independently. However, for the purposes of evaluation/adjustment, updates (in terms of a bias weight and errors) must be

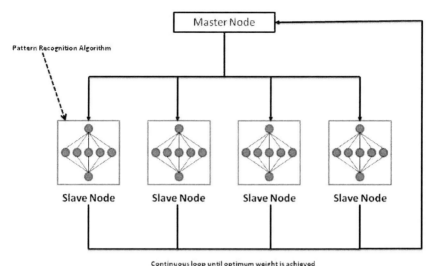

FIGURE 2.5: Distributed pattern recognition based on the process farming approach.

sent to the master node after each cycle. This process is iteratively performed until the optimum bias weight and errors have been achieved by the network. Each processor uses a subset of the training data. Therefore, each processor performs the training procedure on a subset of the overall data.

2. *Pipelining:* The recognition procedure of the pipelining approach follows an incremental method. The training process is conducted subsequently using a pipeline procedure similar to that shown in Figure 2.6. Each processor contains a copy of the algorithm and performs a recognition process on a particular training subset. However, each time the weight and error changes are passed from one processor to another, they are modified, evaluated, and incorporated into each subsequent weight and error calculation.

The top-down approach towards distributed pattern recognition has several limitations including the following:

1. *Recall Disintegrity:* Due to the vertical splitting of data, the distribution of a training data set into a number of subsets can create disintegrity in the training process and influence the actual recall process. The weight changes produced by the algorithm on a highly cohesive training set, i.e.,

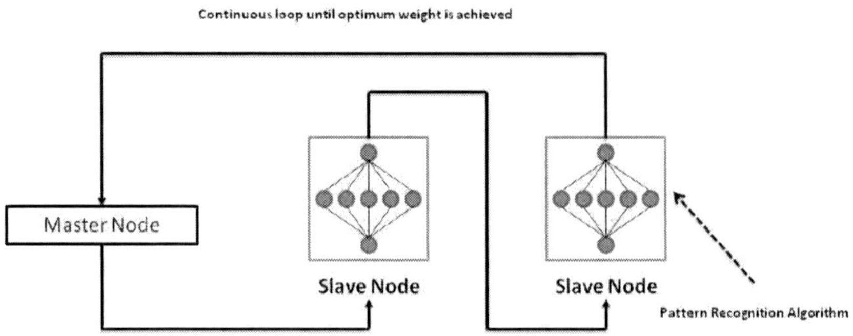

FIGURE 2.6: Distributed pattern recognition based on the process pipelining approach.

training data that is hardly classified due to dissimilar feature values, are significantly different than the weight changes produced on a loosely cohesive data, i.e., data that is easily classified and clustered.

2. *Highly Congestive Network:* In terms of the number of training cycles required to obtain an optimum output, algorithms such as the feed-forward neural network and Hopfield network are highly iterative in nature. A large number of iterations in the training/recognition process will lead to massive communication exchanges within any distributed environment, and thus create a highly congested network.

3. *Unchanged Level of Complexity:* In existing distributed pattern recognition schemes, actual pattern recognition processes are applied at a smaller scale, i.e., similar algorithms are used with a smaller training space. Therefore, the complexity of the algorithm is unchanged. By reducing the amount of training data used, executing recognition processes at a smaller scale may improve the algorithm's performance time. However, the processing time also depends on the number of learning cycles implemented for each recognition process. Though the complexity of the algorithm remains unchanged, it is hard to estimate its resource requirements. Therefore, this approach may not be applicable for resource-constrained networks, such as wireless sensor networks (WSNs).

2.4 Pattern Distribution Techniques

Implementations of existing neural network/machine learning approaches for pattern recognition have shown some limitations. These include the generalization problem and complex learning mechanisms. These limitations affect the scalability of the approaches for real-time and large-scale recognition deployments. Furthermore, existing approaches are CPU-centric, i.e., they have been developed with the single-processing mechanism in mind. According to Ikeda et al. [40], it is difficult for current neural network approaches to implement actual associative memory principles, in which simple low-cost devices are equipped with these algorithms for pattern recognition purposes.

In solving the scalability issue within pattern recognition applications, we intend to shift the recognition paradigm from a sequential-based CPU-centric approach toward a parallel in-network approach. The in-network processing paradigm concentrates on the delegation and distribution of processes over the body of a network rather than utilizing a single-processing device or node. The ability of a system to distribute data across a number of processors or nodes in the network is an important aspect in the distributed approach for pattern recognition. It is essential that pattern distribution techniques be applied. In this section, two different pattern distribution techniques are described:

1. *Subpattern Distribution:* Each pattern is partitioned into subpatterns for recognition over the entire network. Each node within the network receives a subpattern for processing.

2. *Set Distribution:* A pattern set containing a number of patterns is distributed for recognition. Each pattern subset will be executed by a specific processing node within the network.

Figure 2.7 shows a comparison of the techniques. These techniques will be discussed in the following subsections.

2.4.1 Subpattern Distribution

The subpattern distribution technique in the DPR approach involves dividing a pattern into small-scale subpatterns. These subpatterns will be distributed across several processing nodes for the recognition process. The work of Garai and Chaudhuri [25] on the Distributed Hierarchical Genetic Algorithm (DHGA) for efficient optimization and pattern matching is an example of this distribution technique. In this work, the entire search space is divided into subspaces, and the search process is conducted at this level. Parallel genetic algorithms are implemented on each subspace.

Ikeda et al. [40] proposed a distributed approach for Hamming associative memory using the decoupled Hamming AM approach. The input vector is

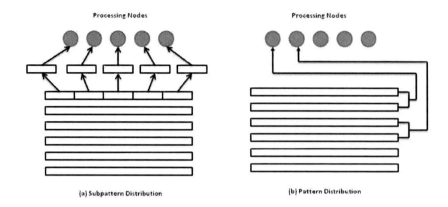

FIGURE 2.7: A comparison between subpattern and pattern subset distribution techniques.

partitioned into a number of modules known as windows. Each window is used in a Hamming memory operation. The recognition results from each Hamming memory are sent to a decision network to determine the final output from the system. Mu et al. [41] extended the decoupled Hamming AM approach by introducing a voting mechanism into the decision-making process.

In addition to the division of the input space into subspaces, pattern distribution techniques include a recognition process that is based on the atomic pattern components that make up the entire pattern representation. For instance, Khan and Mihailescu [2] proposed parallel pattern recognition in a wireless sensor network (WSN) environment using a Graph Neuron (GN) approach. In their work, sensory data obtained from a sensor node was considered to be a component of the entire pattern represented by the network. Subpattern distribution techniques allow recognition process to be performed on minimal data, i.e., due to the size of the subpattern, the complexity is low. Nevertheless, this technique is impossible to deploy in all deterministic approaches. Some algorithms are highly cohesive, and the whole input space must be included in its computations to obtain an optimum result.

2.4.2   Pattern Set Distribution

Pattern set distribution is a common approach in distributed pattern recognition. It involves the distribution of separate input data sets to each of the processing entities within the network.

Patterns are also distributed during the pre-processing stage of the classification/recognition process. For instance, Kokiopoulou and Frossard [42] proposed a distributed support vector machine (SVM) approach for the classification of images within a sensor network. In this method, the input signal is distributed into different feature subspaces. These feature subspaces are pre-processed and sent to a final module that conducts the classification process. This approach alleviates the need for large training data sets for SVM.

Some pattern set distribution techniques also distribute patterns to processing entities within a network. For instance, Lobo, Bandeira, and Moura-Pires [43] proposed a distributed SOM for a ship recognition process using acoustic signatures. This type of technique requires that results are collected from each processing entity and further processed by an intensive post-processing mechanism. The pattern set distribution technique does not minimize the computational complexity of the recognition algorithm. However, it reduces the execution time and allows for parallel processing implementations. This technique is suitable for recognition schemes that analyze a large number of patterns. However, the technique does not fit well into systems that cater to high-dimensional and large-scale data, such as Magnetic Resonance Imaging (MRI) images.

Existing distributed pattern recognition approaches tend to employ the set distribution technique. This technique alleviates the need for a large number of training data sets, which leads to fast learning speeds. Nevertheless, the complexity issue remains unsolved. Examples of DPR schemes that use the set distribution technique include the works carried out in [42, 44, 45].

2.5   Current DPR Schemes

A number of purely distributed pattern recognition approaches have been pursued. Several neural network schemes have been developed that have a distributed processing capability, such as the Hamming AM and Morphological AM. Nevertheless, the algorithmic distribution capability has yet to be further analyzed. In recent years, DPR methods based on the original Graph Neuron (GN) algorithm have been developed. Established extensions include the Hierarchical GN (HGN) [3] and Distributed Hierarchical GN (DHGN) [46] algorithms. In this section, we will discuss briefly some of the fundamental characteristics of these schemes.

2.5.1   Graph Neuron

Graph Neuron (GN) is a pattern recognition algorithm that implements a simple associative memory (AM) architecture, which provides the capability of pattern recall based on similar or incomplete patterns. In an associative memory architecture, the store and recall operations are based on an association with the input rather than the address of the memory content as is used in a conventional memory architecture. Therefore, pattern recognition algorithms that are based on associative memory have higher recognition accuracy than algorithms that implement recognition using a conventional memory architecture. Other associative memory algorithms include the Hopfield network, Kernel Associative Memory (KAM), Morphological Associative Memory (MAM), and Hamming Associative Memory.

In addition to its associative memory architecture, GN follows some characteristics of graph-based pattern recognition algorithms, as demonstrated in [47, 48, 49, 50]. However, GN implements in-network processing, and thus solves the scalability issue encountered in other graph-based pattern recognition algorithms, as described in [51]. According to Nasution [52], the in-network processing capability of GN offers two advantages: 1) it eliminates the computational problems encountered in large patterns and pattern databases and 2) its implementation is ideal for resource-constrained environments, such as event detection in wireless sensor networks (WSNs).

An overview of graph-based algorithms for pattern recognition is presented below. Some of their characteristics were inherited by GN.

2.5.1.1   Graph-Based Pattern Recognition

A graph comprises a set of vertices and edges. Therefore, a graph, G, is represented by $G = (V, E)$, where V is the set of vertices (also known as nodes or points), E represents the edges (also known as lines or arcs), and $E \subset V \times V$. An edge, $e \in E$, connects two vertices, x, and $y \in V$, and is denoted by $e = (x, y)$. Graph vertices and edges can contain one or more pieces of information. If only a single piece of information is available, the graph is called a labeled graph. If more information is contained on vertices or edges, the graph is called an attributed graph. Figure 2.8 shows an example of a labeled graph.

In graph-based pattern recognition, each pattern is represented as a graph. A modeled (or stored) pattern, P_{store}, and an input pattern, P_{input}, are represented by graphs G_{store} and G_{input}, respectively. As described in [53], pattern recognition based on a graph representation follows the graph matching problem: Given $G_{store} = (V_s, E_s)$ and $G_{input} = (V_i, E_i)$, where $|V_s| = |V_i|$, a one-to-one mapping, $f : V_i \to V_s$, exists, such that for any input pattern element $(x, y) \in E_i \iff (f(x), f(y)) \in E_s$. This mapping function implies isomorphism, and G_{input} is said to be isomorphic to G_{store}. This type of problem is known as exact graph matching. If two graphs have different sets of attributes or different numbers of vertices or edges, isomorphism does not occur and an inexact graph matching algorithm is used.

In the field of computer vision, graphs are used to represent images for the purpose of recognition. In graph-based image recognition, regions of an image are represented by vertices, and edges are used to signify relationships between regions. An important issue in graph-based pattern recognition is that the complexity of the algorithm is significantly affected by an increase in either the size or quantity of the pattern stored. According to Caetano et

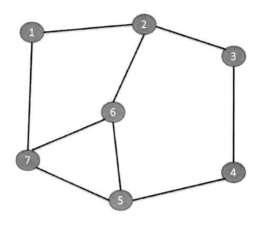

FIGURE 2.8: A labeled graph with a vertex set $V = \{1, 2, 3, 4, 5, 6, 7\}$ and edge set $E = \{\{1, 2\}, \{2, 3\}, \{3, 4\}, \{4, 5\}, \{5, 6\}, \{6, 7\}, \{2, 6\}, \{5, 7\}, \{1, 7\}\}$.

al. [50], the number of possible matches between two graphs grows factorially with the size. Therefore, scalability is an important issue to be resolved.

The in-network processing capability of Graph Neuron eliminates the scalability issue experienced by other graph-based pattern recognition algorithms. General Neuron scales up appropriately with an increase in both pattern size and database. Recognition processes are distributed to a set of processing nodes and processed in parallel. In addition, GN can perform exact and inexact pattern matching based on different sets of attributes. The GN architecture and some implementations will be discussed further in Chapter 3.

2.5.2 Hierarchical Graph Neuron

The Hierarchical Graph Neuron (HGN) [3] implements a one-shot memorization and recall operation using a novel distributed algorithm. The HGN is an enhancement to the graph neuron (GN) algorithm. This improved scheme recognizes incomplete or noisy patterns. The HGN filters noise and crosstalk out of the patter data input by linking multiple GN networks, which resolves the crosstalk problem (see Section 3.4) encountered in closely matched patterns. The HGN scheme is a lightweight, in-network processing algorithm that does not require expensive floating point computations. It is very suitable for real-time applications and tiny devices, such as wireless sensor networks. The HGN can perform direct pattern matching procedures, and the short response time is insensitive to increases in the number of stored patterns. Moreover, the HGN does not require that the operator define rules or set thresholds to achieve the desired results nor does it require heuristics, which entail iterative operations for memorization and pattern recall.

2.5.3   Distributed Hierarchical Graph Neuron

The Distributed Hierarchical Graph Neuron (DHGN) [46] is a parallel associative memory-based pattern recognition algorithm that extends the functionalities and capabilities of the GN algorithm. It is a single-cycle learning algorithm that has an in-network processing capability. By efficiently disseminating recognition processes across the network, the algorithm is able to reduce computational loads [54]. Therefore, it is suitable for deployment in wireless sensor networks and other fine-grained computational networks. In addition, DHGN can be deployed as a recognition engine for large-scale data-processing on coarse-grained networks, such as computational grids and clouds [55, 56].

2.6   Resource Considerations for DPR Implementations

Neural networks designed as processing schemes for pattern recognition applications have inspired many to attempt their deployment in a physical computational network, such as grid and local networks. The fundamental principles of in-network distributed processing for complex computations have been established by the methods used to communicate inputs and outputs between processing nodes. Nevertheless, there are several issues that need to be addressed when an in-network approach is used to deploy complex algorithms. These issues include resource considerations and incurred communication costs.

Current approaches for implementing pattern recognition algorithms in distributed environments have focused on improving the performance time and providing scalability in response to increasing data size and dimension. Nevertheless, these approaches are overburdened by their highly complex computations and require significant resources to perform in a distributed manner. For example, the computational complexity of a recognition process using a Hopfield network with n neurons on a single processor is equivalent to $O(n \log n)$. For the algorithm to exhibit peak performance, it is important that the network acquire sufficient computational resources. However, not all types of computational networks available in the current technological climate can acquire sufficient resources.

Resource-awareness is an important aspect absent from existing DPR schemes. Because the granularities of networks differ, it is essential for the computational and storage costs incurred by a distributed scheme are considered. With available applications ranging from complex data mining processes to event detection, distributed systems have been applied in day-to-day operations ranging from high performance computing networks to lightweight and resource-constrained WSNs. To provide expandable coverage for different types of applications, a dynamic and robust distributed pattern recognition scheme must be able to perform under different network granularities.

2.6.1 Resource-Aware Approach

Resource considerations for conventional and distributed pattern recognition are distinctly different. In a distributed approach, the system must be able to utilize the available resources effectively and efficiently. To ensure proper utilization and communication of resources between processing nodes, a communication model needs to be considered.

Distributed pattern recognition (DPR) has the capability to scale up the process when the size of the problem increases. However, scalability depends on resource availability within a particular computational network. Resource availability is influenced by the capacity and stability of the computational network.

The network capacity of distributed applications, such as DPR, can be viewed in terms of the granularity of the network. Commonly, computational networks take the form of a coarse-grained network, such as grid computing, or a fine-grained network, such as a wireless sensor network (WSN). The processing capacity and capability of these networks may differ. Because application deployment tends to focus on a single problem domain, most existing DPR schemes are unable to adapt to different network granularities. Nevertheless, some DPR schemes, such as the DHGN, have been developed with adaptive network granularity considerations [4] and can be deployed in both coarse- and fine-grained networks.

In addition to capacity, the stability of a computational network plays an important role in determining its resource availability. A stable network is defined as a network with minimal or no resource interference resulting from fault or error occurrences. For a particular application, such as DPR, to perform its function with minimal or no interruptions, a fault tolerance mechanism needs to be considered.

2.6.2 Message-Passing Model in DPR

Process communication plays an important role in any distributed system and determines how efficiently a system adapts to different network configurations and characteristics. Processes can be communicated within a network using message exchanges between processing nodes. In any distributed system, each processing node might require data exchange with other nodes to complete a specific task or process. A thorough analysis of inter-process communication must be performed to ensure that the proposed system is capable of handling different network conditions. Similarly, the process communication aspects of the distributed algorithms being proposed require significant consideration.

A number of inter-process communication models have been developed in recent years. These models include message-passing, shared memory, and mobile agent. These models aid in the understanding of the communication procedures occurring within a computational network. Message-passing is an inter-process communication model developed as a guideline for process cooperation between computing nodes in a parallel environment. This model is based on a set of fundamental principles including:

1. Each process has its own local memory.

2. Processes communicate their data using a message exchange structure (sending and receiving messages).

3. The transfer of data requires cooperative operations between each process involved, i.e., each send operation must have a corresponding receive operation.

The cooperative operations in the message-passing model address how communication is being conducted between processing nodes within a network. These operations form the components of a message-passing library, which in return are used in the implementation of message-passing communication. Examples of message-passing libraries include the Message Passing Library (MPL) introduced for IBM SP2, the Parallel Virtual Machine (PVM), and Message Passing Interface (MPI). The MPI library provides extensive portability and can be deployed on different types of platforms. The MPI specification for message-passing has been established as a standard. An enhancement of MPI standard, known as MPI-2, offers dynamic task control and a functional parallel I/O capability [57]. Further discussions on this message-passing model are included in Chapter 6.

Part II

Evolution of Internet-Scale Recognition

Chapter 3

One-Shot Learning Considerations

An interesting area of current research focuses on developing capabilities of smart objects, such as sensors to do complex processing beyond simple data collection, including mechanisms for energy conservation, in lightweight devices. Sensors that are able to perform recognition or clustering of events in situ minimize the communication time between sensors and controlling devices, such as the base station, and thus improve the performance of the entire network at a large-scale. Such capabilities are limited by the complex computation requirements of existing recognition or clustering algorithms, such as highly iterative training, frequent weight adjustments, and an inability to perform data distribution for large-scale processing.

One-shot learning is a type of learning mechanism that was inspired by the ability of biological systems, such as a human being, to recognize objects at a single glance [37]. It is estimated that a child has learned almost all of the 10,000 to 30,000 object categories by the age of six. Data can be recognized or clustered quickly and efficiently if objects can be recognized without having to iteratively memorize its characteristics or features.

One-shot learning was developed as a mechanism for systems to learn information with a minimal amount of initial data. In the artificial, computational world, the key motivation and intuition for one-shot learning is that systems, like humans, can use prior information of object categories to learn and classify new objects.

An important characteristic that differentiates one-shot learning from other styles of learning is the emphasis on the principle of knowledge transfer, which encapsulates prior knowledge of learned categories and allows for learning on minimal training examples [58]. The question remaining to be answered is how this might be achieved. According to Lake et al. [59], one hypothesis is that the sharing of partial knowledge is core to one-shot learning. This type of learning through inference is also used in the Graph Neuron (GN) implementation by Khan and Mihailescu [2]. In GN, patterns are stored based on the similarities of adjacent pattern elements within a particular pattern. These similarities are stored and are the basis of comparison for incoming patterns. In a work conducted by Bart and Ullman [60], a one-shot learning scheme was carried out using selected features that were derived from the learned classification tasks performed in prior learning.

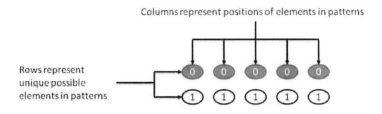

FIGURE 3.1: A two-dimensional GN network for a binary pattern of size five bits.

In this chapter, we will discuss the aspects of one-shot learning and its applicability in DPR applications. This discussion will also include the systems and network considerations for a DPR deployment using a one-shot learning approach. In addition, this chapter will further describe the Graph Neuron (GN) approach (see Section 2.5.1), a one-shot learning DPR scheme designed for WSN implementations [2, 34].

3.1 One-Shot Learning Graph Neuron (GN) Scheme

A GN network is built using a composition of inter-connected processing nodes, known as Graph Neurons (GNs), which follow the size and dimension of a given pattern. In its simplest form, a GN network forms a two-dimensional array of neurons. Each neuron is labeled with a value and position, i.e., a column and row position. Figure 3.1 shows a GN network with a two-dimensional array formation.

A GN network receives an input and stores or processes the input according to the instruction received. Creating a method capable of parallel, in-network processing was an emphasis in the development of the GN method. In contrast, other recognition algorithms are most often implemented using CPU-sequential processing. The parallel, in-network processing capability allows GN to perform fast recognition regardless of the size of the input patterns. Furthermore, by disseminating patterns into pattern elements and distributing them across the network, the storage capacity of this approach is high. According to Nasution [52], the GN algorithm was developed based on the hypothesis that changing the design emphasis from high-speed sequential CPU processing to parallel network centric processing will result in a better associative memory resource.

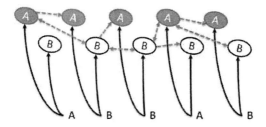

FIGURE 3.2: GN network activation from input pattern *"ABBAB."*

3.1.1   Pattern Representation

The GN pattern representation follows the representation of patterns in other graph-matching based algorithms described in the previous subsection. Each neuron in the network holds an information pair, *(value, position)*, which contains information about the elements that constitute the pattern. In correspondence with the graph-based structure, each neuron acts as a vertex that holds pattern element information in the form of a value or identification (ID). The adjacency communication between two or more neurons is represented by the edge of a graph. Message communications in a GN network are restricted to adjacent neurons (of the array). As described in Khan et al. [31], if the number of neurons in the network increases, there is not a corresponding increase in the communication. Figure 3.2 shows a two-dimensional GN graph-based structure for a given input pattern. Note that only GNs that have a matched pattern element and position will be activated and perform communication with its adjacent neurons. This self-organization creates links between neurons and builds up pattern information in the network.

Each neuron in the same row holds a similar ID or value, but their positions (column position) differ within the network, as shown in Figure 3.2. These value assignments uniquely mark the position of each neuron with its column number in the network. This type of arrangement is just one of the possible structural neuron arrangements of the network. Neuron arrangement will be discussed further in later chapters. To determine the positions of other neurons, each neuron within the network must be able to obtain information pertaining to the size of the network. For recognition processes, this information is important in identifying adjacent neurons.

An input pattern for a GN network might be a signal spike, or stimulus resulting from user activation or information derived from an executable program or sensory device. In addition, it might represent bit elements of an image [61] or a stimulus/signal spike produced in a network intrusion detection application [34]. Each neuron is able to identify its ID from the pattern that has been introduced. For instance, a GN that holds the value *"B"* will only respond to a pattern signal that has element *"B"* in the same position. To generate the network that matches the criteria of the patterns that will be used, a GN network must be able to obtain prior knowledge of the pattern. This type of network is a supervised GN network.

3.1.2 Recognition Procedure

The GN recognition process involves the memorization of adjacency information obtained from the edges of the graph. Adjacency information for each GN is represented using the *(left, right)* formation. Each activated neuron records the information retrieved from its adjacent left or right neuron. In the GN terminology, this adjacency information is known as a bias entry, and each neuron maintains an array of bias entries. The entries for the entire stored pattern are collectively stored in the bias arrays. Each neuron holds a single bias array, which contains all of the bias entries obtained in recognition processes. Because each neuron is only required to store a single array, the storage complexity of the GN recognition process is low. Furthermore, the bias array of each neuron stores only the unique adjacency information derived from the input patterns.

In the graph-matching representation, pattern recognition based on a GN network implements the graph comparison approach by treating each pattern as a graph, each element of a pattern as a vertex, and the position between elements as an edge. Consider the following example: Given two patterns, P_{in} and P_{st}, P_{in} is said to match P_{st} if the following conditions are satisfied:

1. The number of vertices in P_{in}, V_{in}, is equivalent to the number of vertices in P_{st}, V_{st}, i.e., $|V_{in}| = |V_{st}|$.

2. The number of edges in P_{in}, E_{in} is equivalent to the number of edges in P_{st}, E_{st}, i.e., $|E_{in}| = |E_{st}|$.

3. The bias entry, $b \in B_{in}$ for each vertex $v \in V_{in}$ is a subset of bias array, B_{st}, for each vertex $v \in V_{st}$, i.e., $b \in B_{st}$.

The pattern recognition process initially takes place in the following phases:

3.1.2.1 Pattern input phase

An input pattern, defined by p *(value, position)* pairs, is sequentially broadcast throughout the network. Each neuron responds only to the input pair that corresponds to the pre-defined position and value settings of the neuron; it disregards the remainder of the pattern. From Figure 3.3, *GN X(1)* has a pre-defined value = *"X"* and position = *1* and will respond to the first letter of pattern *P1*, i.e., *"X"YXX*, which is input as pair *p1(X,1)*. This neuron will ignore the rest of the message. Similarly, *GN Y(2)* will respond to the second pair *p2(Y,2)*; *GN X(3)* will respond to *p3(X,3)*; and *GN X(4)* will respond

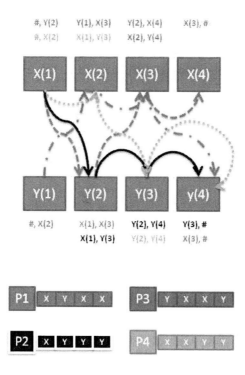

FIGURE 3.3: Illustration of the bias array in a GN recognition process for different input patterns.

to *p4(X,4)*. All other neurons will remain inactive during this pattern input phase.

3.1.2.2 Synchronization phase

A broadcast signal is sent to all of the neurons to mark the end of the incoming pattern.

3.1.2.3 Bias array update

During this phase, each activated neuron contacts its adjacent nodes to learn which nodes responded to the input. As shown in Figure 3.3, for the input pattern *P1 (XYXX)*, *GN X(1)* will update its local bias array with the entry *[GN Y(2)]*. Similarly, *GN Y(2)* will update its bias array with the entry *[GN X(1), GN X(3)]*; *GN X(3)* will add *[GN Y(2), GN X(4)]* to its bias array; and *GN X(4)* will add *[GN X(3)]*. Each bias array entry records

TABLE 3.1: Store and Recall Responses of a GN Array

Input Sequence	Input Pattern	Output
First	*XXYX*	*#### (Store)*
Second	*XXYX*	*XXYX (Recall)*

the adjacent nodes that are activated in a particular pattern input phase. A row of the bias array represents a part of the stored pattern. A bias entry is defined if the set of adjacent neurons does not match any existing rows of the bias array. A new pattern is found when at least one activated neuron cannot find a matching entry in its bias array. In this stage, new patterns are stored, and previously encountered patterns are recalled. Table 3.1 shows the process when pattern *"XXYX"* is stored and then recalled. Note that when a pattern is stored for the first time, the output from the GN network is a null entry, represented by the *"#"* pattern in the table. A null response indicates that no match was found, and the segments of the pattern were stored by the GN array.

Stages 1 and 2 of the GN learning phase take place in a completely parallel and decentralized manner. As shown in Figure 3.3, the maximum size of a bias array is two and occurs in *GN (Y,2)* after the array has stored four patterns. Scalability tests, using as many as 16,384 nodes, have shown that increases in the size of the network result in nominal increases in the computational complexity [33].

In the supervised GN approach, the size of the network depends on the size of the patterns and the number of unique elements in the pattern used for recognition or classification purposes. Given pattern $P = a$, the number of GNs, $N(a)$, required in a one-dimensional GN network analysis is given as follows.

$$N(a) = s_a \bullet e_a \qquad (3.1)$$

where s_a represents the size, and e_a is the number of unique elements of pattern a. Eventually, an increase in the dimensions of the patterns will increase the number of GNs in the GN network. Therefore, given the dimension of pattern a as d_a, the number of GNs can be determined as follows.

$$N(a) = s_a \bullet e_a \bullet d_a \qquad (3.2)$$

The GN approach has been used in a number of applications involving pattern recognition and classification. With lightweight and distributed features, GN implementations have been applied in resource-constrained networks, such as wireless sensor networks (WSNs). Khan and Mihailescu [2] proposed a GN implementation for pattern recognition in a WSN. A simulation of sensory reactions on an artificial nervous system using a WSN showed that the GN approach is able to differentiate between internal stress patterns in the network and patterns that result from external loading conditions in a structural health monitoring (SHM) application. In addition, the data storage capacity requirements of a GN are low. Therefore, GN is most suitable for a WSN deployment. Baig et al. [34] proposed using a GN pattern recognition algorithm to detect a distributed denial of service (DDoS) attack in a WSN. The GN algorithm was able to detect DDoS attack patterns in a WSN by analyzing the internal traffic flow of the network. This implementation of a GN has been tested on three different network topologies, and the results have shown that it produces high recognition accuracies for all topologies.

The GN algorithm also offers an energy-efficient mechanism for pattern recognition. This follows the work of Baqer and Khan [62] on energy-efficient pattern recognition approaches for WSNs. In their work, event detection based on the GN was demonstrated. By conducting the detection and analysis in situ, i.e., at the sensor node level, the GN was shown to offer an energy-efficient mechanism for event detection in WSNs. This is in contrast to existing approaches, which perform the analysis at the base station.

The ability of the Graph Neuron (GN) algorithm to provide a fast, efficient and scalable solution for pattern recognition makes it suitable for deployment in a number of different network environments ranging from resource-constrained networks, such as WSNs, to large-scale networks, such as the Internet and peer-to-peer (P2P) networks. Nevertheless, a GN implementation has its own limitations, including a large number of required neurons in large-scale and multi-dimensional patterns and inaccuracies introduced by a phenomenon known as the intersection or crosstalk problem. Given that the structure of a GN network can be abstracted in the form of memory structure or actual processing nodes working together to form a GN network, the first limitation is less significant. The intersection problem is an important limitation of the GN algorithm. This problem is a result of GN's inability to obtain full pattern information. The GN builds up pattern information using links between adjacent neurons. Learning or adapting information by means of adjacency relationships between neurons is known as the comparative-collaboration technique for one-shot learning.

3.2 One-Shot Learning Model

Graph Neuron implements a one-shot learning approach in its recognition procedure. In this learning approach, learning occurs collaboratively between nodes rather than independently by each processing node, as is implemented

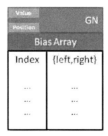

FIGURE 3.4: Abstract representation of a GN and its storage framework.

in methods such as Hebbian and incremental learning. The term used for this collaborative learning is *Collaborative-Comparison Learning (CCL)* [63].

3.2.1   Bias Array Design for Pattern Memorization

In a GN-based implementation, patterns are stored as associations between the elements of the pattern. This pattern representation is different from other neural network approaches, which store patterns as a composition of values. The pattern storage mechanism adopted by GN is a bias array. Figure 3.4 shows an abstract representation of a GN and its storage structure.

GN minimizes the storage required for input patterns. For one-dimensional input patterns, the growth of the storage element of each neuron is limited by the *Index{left, right}* format of a bias entry. Consider a comparison between a GN bias entry and the storage capacity requirements of each neuron in a feed-forward neural network, given different binary pattern sizes used in the networks. In a feed-forward network, each neuron requires input from all of the elements within a pattern. When given a pattern, p with n input elements (i.e., the size) and d dimensions, each neuron must memorize d^n combinations of patterns. Conversely, the storage capacity required for memorization by each neuron in a GN network is only d^2. From this perspective, GN offers significantly higher storage efficiency than the feed-forward neural network.

3.2.2   Collaborative-Comparison Learning Technique

In a GN-based implementation, an adjacency comparison approach is employed in the learning scheme using simple signal/data comparisons. Each GN holds a segment of the overall subpattern. Collectively, these neurons represent the entire subpattern. Consider the GN subnet structure shown in Figure 3.5. The entire *"ABCDE"* pattern can be stored using five GNs, each responsible for capturing the values of its adjacent neurons. By linking these neurons into a one-dimensional structure, we can determine the GNs that collaboratively contain a memory of the *"ABCDE"* pattern.

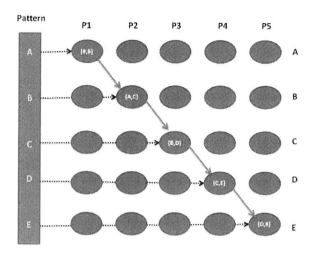

FIGURE 3.5: Collaborative-comparison learning approach for the one-dimensional pattern *"ABCDE."* Each activated graph neuron (GN) stores the signals received from its adjacent neurons.

The collaborative-comparison learning approach compares an external input pattern to the stored entries of each neuron's bias array, which is a local data structure containing the history of adjacent node activation. Each neuron learns by comparing the signals from its adjacent neighbors and the recorded entries within its memory, i.e., the bias array. A bias array $\sigma = \{s_1, s_2, \ldots, s_x\}$, comprises signal entries, s_i for $i \in x$. If the external signal set matches any of the stored entries, i.e., $s_{ext} \in \sigma$, the bias index, i, of the matched s_i will be recalled. Otherwise, the signal will be added into the memory as s_{x+1}. There are two advantages to using this approach: 1) the bias array design for pattern storage minimizes the data storage requirement and 2) all types of data can be processed. For instance, the signal can be data vectors or frequency signals, and thus spatial and temporal data can be accommodated. In addition, the collaborative-comparison learning technique does not require the synaptic plasticity rule used by other learning mechanisms, such as Hebbian and incremental learning. Thus, new patterns are learned without affecting previously stored information.

3.3   GN Complexity Estimation

An estimate of the computational complexity of the recognition procedure of a GN implementation follows. A Big-O analysis of the bias array update phase of the GN procedure was performed. Because the core recognition function in the GN procedure is the bias array update of each GN, a limited analysis is justified. The pseudocode for the bias array update procedure for each neuron is as follows:

Algorithm 1 Bias Array Update Procedure for a GN

1:   $input.l \leftarrow leftGN$
2:   $input.r \leftarrow rightGN$
3:   **for all** $\sigma_{l,r} \in \sigma$ **do**
4:     **if** $input_{l,r} \equiv \sigma_{l,r}$ **then**
5:       **return** $\sigma_{l,r}$
6:       exit FOR
7:     **else**
8:       **if** $\sigma_{l,r}$ is last entry **then**
9:         $\sigma_{l,r} + 1 = input_{l,r}$
10:      **else**
11:        continue
12:      **end if**
13:     **end if**
14: **end for**

Consider the bias array update as a function $f(\sigma) = T_{f(\sigma)}(N)$. Algorithm 1 clearly demonstrates that the function implements a linear search mechanism for each input pattern, and thus its complexity is $O(N)$. We can deduce that $T_{f(\sigma)}(N) = O(N)$. By implementing a simple linear search technique to identify recall or introduce new patterns into the network, the Big-O analysis proves that GN offers a low complexity recognition process.

A storage capacity analysis provides another complexity estimate for the GN implementation. This analysis estimates the maximum size of the bias array for each input pattern stored in the GN network. For a two-dimensional GN structure, the maximum number of bias entries is determined by the number of possible combinations of *(left, right)* entries σ_{ent}, obtained from adjacent neurons. The number of possible combinations is directly related to the number of rows (or pattern elements) in the composition. In addition, the maximum bias array size for each neuron depends on its position. For a given number of rows, n_{row}, there are two possible values for the maximum bias array size, $\sigma_{\max}$ of a neuron:

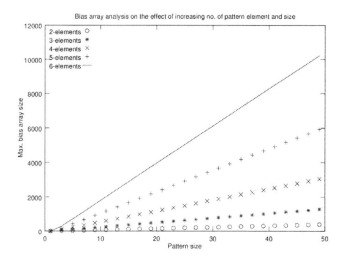

FIGURE 3.6: Maximum bias array size analysis for a GN implementation as a function of pattern size. The results for several numbers of different pattern elements are shown.

1. If the neuron is at the edge, $\sigma_{\max,e} = n_{row}$.

2. For a non-edge neuron, $\sigma_{\max,ne} = n_{row}^2$.

For a pattern of size, $S = a$, the total maximum bias array capacity for all neurons in the network, $\max \sigma$, can be estimated using the following equation:

$$\begin{aligned}
\max \sigma &= n_{row} \times \left(\sigma_{\max,ne} \times (a - 2) + 2\sigma_{\max,e} \right) \\
&= n_{row} \times \left(n_{row}^2 \times (a - 2) + 2n_{row} \right) \\
&= n_{row}^2 \times \left(n_{row} \times (a - 2) + 2 \right)
\end{aligned} \quad (3.3)$$

The total maximum bias array capacity of a one-dimensional GN network is significantly affected by the number of different elements in the input patterns. However, the size of the pattern only moderately influences the maximum capacity. In this context, large-scale patterns with minimum variation between elements will have a lower impact on the bias array capacity than large-scale patterns with high variation between elements. Figure 3.6 shows the growth of the total bias array size for a GN network as a function of the number of different pattern elements and pattern size.

The total maximum bias array size grows linearly with pattern size. In this regard, the GN network has proven to offer scalability for large-scale patterns. An increase in the dimension of the patterns also affects the total size of the bias array. This is due to an increase in the number of possible combinations of entries. For instance, in a three-dimensional GN network, the bias entry of each neuron is *(left, right, top, bottom)*, which is equivalent to n_{row}^4.

3.4   Graph Neuron Limitations

The GN pattern recognition approach exchanges subpattern information between two or more adjacent neurons. For instance, a GN network will memorize the pattern *"abcdef"* in the form of subpatterns: *"ab," "abc," "bcd," "cde," "def,"* and *"ef."* Note that the number of subpatterns is equivalent to the number of active neurons.

The GN's limited awareness of the overall pattern affects the accuracy of its recognition scheme. As the size of the pattern increases, it is more difficult for a GN network to obtain an overview of the pattern's composition. Different patterns that have a similar subpattern structure lead to false recall and incomplete results. Let us suppose that a GN network can allocate six possible element values, e.g., *"u," "v," "w," "x," "y,"* and *"z,"* for a five-element pattern. The pattern *"uvwxz"* is introduced, followed by *"zvwxy."* These two patterns are stored by the GN array. Next, we introduce the pattern *"uvwxy"*; this will produce a recall. Because the last pattern does not match the previously stored patterns, the recall is false. The reason for this false recall is that a GN only knows of its own value and the values of its adjacent neurons. The input patterns are stored as the segments *"uv," "uvw," "vwx," "wxy,"* and *"xy."* The last input pattern, though different from the two previous patterns, comprises the segments also found in previously stored patterns. Figure 3.7 uses a graphical representation to simplify this example.

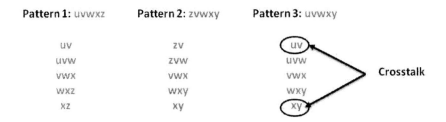

FIGURE 3.7: An illustration of the crosstalk phenomenon for patterns input to a GN network.

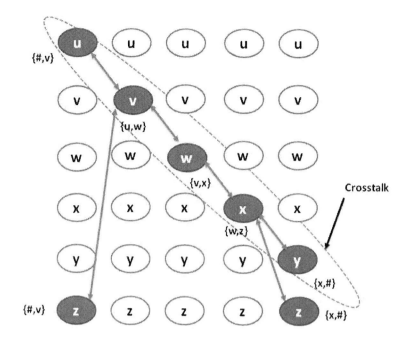

FIGURE 3.8: Crosstalk phenomenon in GN pattern recognition.

The example is extended by analyzing the bias array of the GN network for the example given previously. Figure 3.8 shows an illustration of the bias array analysis of the GN network for the crosstalk example. Note that the recall made for pattern *"uvwxy"* is perceived to be true by all of the activated neurons because all the subpatterns are found. However, the actual recall is inaccurate because the test pattern as a whole does not match the stored patterns. This phenomenon is known as intersection or crosstalk problem.

In Figure 3.8, the bias arrays for patterns *"uvwxz"* and *"zvwxy"* are stored. When the *"uvwxy"* pattern is introduced, all of the bias entries of the two original patterns are recalled, and thus a false recall is created.

The inability of the GN algorithm to obtain an overview of the entire pattern leads to false recalls. A mechanism to eliminate this problem needs to be devised. Nasution and Khan [3] suggested a hierarchical GN implementation. In the next chapter, we will discuss the algorithmic design and implementation of the hierarchical GN model. We will also analyze the complexity of the model and the recognition accuracy of the pattern classification.

3.5 Significance of One-Shot Learning

In this chapter, one-shot learning was presented. The significance of a learning mechanism in an Internet-scale environment cannot be understated. Current pattern recognition implementations cannot deny that the recognition efficiency can adapt to an increasing scale of data through this one-shot learning mechanism. A scheme that can implement learning using the fewest number of possible steps is admirable. An example of such a scheme, Graph Neuron pattern recognition, was presented. Although the implementation has limitations, we believe that the concept should be further explored and its capabilities extended.

Chapter 4

Hierarchical Model for Pattern Recognition

The computational complexity of neural network algorithms is an important factor in determining the effectiveness and efficiency of a pattern recognition scheme. The computational resource requirements, such as processing time and memory space, are heavily impacted by increases in the computational complexity. Therefore, an increase in the size and/or the dimensionality of the patterns disproportionately affects the computational resource requirement. As mentioned in Chapter 1, size and dimensionality are two key aspects in Internet-scale pattern recognition. Internet-scale pattern recognition can be defined as the recognition process for large-scale data. It has been influenced by the development of sophisticated data-harvesting techniques and growth in data storage technologies.

In Chapter 2, the theoretical background of the distributed pattern recognition (DPR) scheme and some examples of DPR implementations were presented. A one-shot learning mechanism is considered important in the design of effective and scalable DPR schemes. In Chapter 3, we presented the Graph Neuron (GN) algorithm, a DPR scheme that uses one-shot learning. This fast learning approach distributes learning using the adjacency comparison approach. A discussion of the limitations of the GN algorithm, including false recalls generated by the crosstalk problem, was also presented.

In this chapter, the discussion of a GN-based DPR scheme will be extended. This chapter will elaborate on the details of the hierarchical concept and model for a GN implementation. The hierarchical approach eliminates the crosstalk problem of the single-layer GN scheme. The effects of a hierarchical structure on the complexity and scalability of the DPR scheme will also be discussed.

4.1 Evolution of One-Shot Learning: The Hierarchical Approach

To solve the crosstalk problem in the GN pattern recognition algorithm, Nasution and Khan [3] proposed a hierarchical structure for GN, known as the Hierarchical Graph Neuron (HGN). The guiding principle for the development

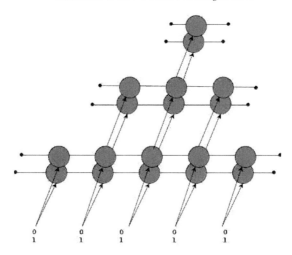

FIGURE 4.1: The layout of a Hierarchical Graph Neuron (HGN) for a binary pattern of size 5 bits.

of the HGN was to expand the capability of *"perceiving neighbors"* within the network. This was achieved by adding higher layers of GNs that see all of the pattern information and provide a bird's eye view of the overall pattern. Figure 4.1 shows the hierarchical layout of the HGN for a binary pattern of size 5 bits.

Figure 4.1 demonstrates that the HGN comprises of layers of GN networks arranged in a pyramid-like formation. This arrangement holds all of the information related to the structure of the patterns stored in the network. The HGN network, as shown in Figure 4.1, is only used in pattern recognition applications involving one-dimensional patterns. However, the HGN does not limit the dimensionality of patterns. For applications that involve complex patterns, the HGN can be expanded to two, three, or even multi-dimensional hierarchies. Figure 4.2 shows examples of an HGN composition for a two-dimensional pattern of size 49 (7 × 7) and a three-dimensional pattern of size 147 (7 × 7 × 3). For simplicity, several pattern elements have been omitted from this figure.

There is an interesting side effect to increasing the dimensions of an HGN network. According to Nasution [52], an increase in the dimension of the hierarchical composition leads to a significant reduction in the number of GNs in the hierarchy. This behavior improves the efficiency of the network for large-scale patterns. For example, given a one-dimensional pattern of size 147, the total number of GNs required is: 147 + 145 + 143 + ... + 3 + 1 = 5476. A two-dimensional (21 × 7 = 147) GN composition requires: 21 × 7 + 21 × 5 + 21 × 3 + 21 + 19 + ... + 3 + 1 = 436 GNs. In this example, increasing the dimensionality by 1 led to a 92% reduction in the number of

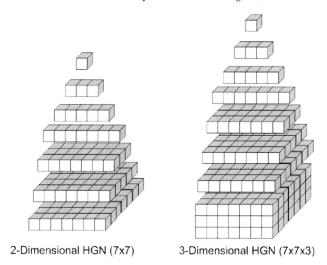

2-Dimensional HGN (7x7)   3-Dimensional HGN (7x7x3)

FIGURE 4.2: HGN composition for two- and three-dimensional patterns of size 49 and 147, respectively.

GNs in the composition. Higher dimensional structures have a significantly smaller network size.

As discussed in the previous chapter, pattern representation in a GN network applies the graph-based *(value, position)* structure. The HGN implementation follows a similar approach. In addition to *(value, position)*, the HGN requires the size of the patterns. Patterns used in the HGN recognition scheme must have an odd-size length. This requirement caters to the hierarchical structure of the HGN network and results in one top neuron which sees the overall pattern structure. Patterns with an even-size length must add a *"dummy"* value at the end of the pattern.

4.1.1   Solution to Crosstalk Problem

The main limitation of the Graph Neuron implementation, the intersection or crosstalk issue, is attributed to its inability to see the entire pattern structure. This limitation has been overcome by the hierarchical GN network layout of the HGN. In this subsection, further analysis of this solution will be presented.

A one-dimensional HGN network for patterns of size 5 bits, shown in Figure 4.3, will be considered. For six different pattern elements, the number of GNs required for this composition is $6 \times ((5 + 1) \div 2)^2 = 54$.

When the pattern *"uvwxz"* is introduced into the HGN network, each GN that has a *(value, position)* that matches an element in the pattern will be activated. Therefore, GNs $U1$, $V2$, $W3$, $X4$, and $Z5$ will be activated. Once activated, each base layer GN executes a recognition process by exchanging

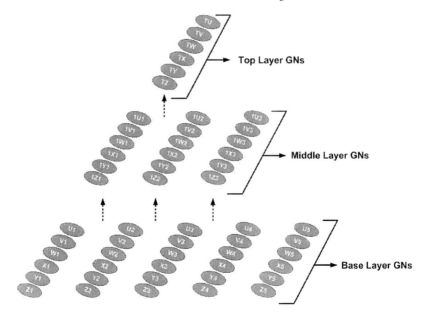

FIGURE 4.3: HGN composition for crosstalk example (see Figure 3.8).

its value with the adjacent GNs. The resulting bias array structure is shown in Table 4.1. All active, non-edge GNs ($V2$, $W3$, and $X4$) will send their bias index to their corresponding GN in the higher layer (in this case, $V2 \rightarrow 1V1$, $W3 \rightarrow 1W2$, and $X4 \rightarrow 1X3$). Once a layer-1 GN receives a bias index, it is activated. The recognition process at this level compares the base level bias indices received by adjacent layer-1 GNs. The bias array contents of each GN in layer-1 are also shown in Table 4.1. The active, non-edge GN, $1W2$, sends its index to the top layer GN, TW. At this stage, TW checks its bias array for an appearance of the index retrieved from $1W2$. If it appears in the bias array, TW will recall the index and propagate it back to all GNs in the network. Otherwise, a new index will be generated and propagated to the network. Tables 4.2 and 4.3 show the bias arrays obtained when patterns "*zvwxy*" and "*uvwxy*" are introduced into the network.

In the HGN implementation, pattern "*uvwxy*" was found to be different from patterns "*uvwxz*" and "*zvwxy*." Therefore, the crosstalk problem is solved by this hierarchical scheme.

4.1.2 Computational Design for a Hierarchical One-Shot Learning DPR Scheme

The hierarchical composition of a GN network is built up by layers of neurons. The size of the HGN network is important in constructing an efficient composition that is based on the availability and capacity of the processing

TABLE 4.1: Bias Array Entries for All Active GN in the HGN Composition Illustrated in Figure 4.3 When the Pattern *"uvwxz"* Is Introduced

Layer	Active GN	Bias Array Entries
Base	U1	1(#, V2)
	V2	1(U1, W3)
	W3	1(V2, X4)
	X4	1(W3, Z5)
	Z5	1(X4, #)
Middle	1V1	1(#, 1, 1)
	1W2	1(1, 1, 1)
	1X3	1(1, 1, #)
Top	TW	1

TABLE 4.2: Bias Array Entries for All Active GN in the HGN Composition Illustrated in Figure 4.3 When the Pattern *"zvwxy"* Is Introduced

Layer	Active GN	Bias Array Entries
Base	Z1	1(#, V2)
	V2	1(U1, W3) 2(Z1, W3)
	W3	1(V2, X4)
	X4	1(W3, Z5) 2(W3, Y5)
	Y5	1(X4, #)
Middle	1V1	1(#, 1, 1) 2(#, 2, 1)
	1W2	1(1, 1, 1) 2(2, 1, 2)
	1X3	1(1, 1, #) 2(1, 2, #)
Top	TW	1 2

TABLE 4.3: Bias Array Entries for All Active GN in the HGN Composition Illustrated in Figure 4.3 When the Pattern *"uvwxy"* Is Introduced

Layer	Active GN	Bias Array Entries
Base	U1	1(#, V2)
	V2	1(U1, W3) 2(Z1, W3)
	W3	1(V2, X4)
	X4	1(W3, Z5) 2(W3, Y5)
	Y5	1(X4, #)
Middle	1V1	1(#, 1, 1) 2(#, 2, 1)
	1W2	1(1, 1, 1) 2(2, 1, 2) 3(1, 1, 2)
	1X3	1(1, 1, #) 2(1, 2, #)
Top	TW	1 2 3

nodes in a physical network. As mentioned previously, the patterns used in the HGN recognition scheme must be odd-size patterns. Therefore, the base layer of the HGN network must also fulfill this requirement. To analyze the number of neurons required for an HGN network to conduct recognition on patterns of size S, we use and extend the methods described in [52].

In HGN pattern recognition, the number of neurons required to process one-dimensional patterns of size $S = x$ comprising v different pattern elements, $n(x)$, is obtained from the following equation:

$$n(x) = vx + v(x-2) + v(x-4) + \ldots + v$$

$$n(x) = v \sum_{i=0}^{\left(\frac{x-1}{2}\right)} (x - 2i) \tag{4.1}$$

$$n(x) = v \left(\frac{x+1}{2}\right)^2$$

For two-dimensional patterns of size $S = x \times y$, the number of neurons required, $n(x, y)$, is obtained as follows:

$$n(x, y) = xy + (x - 2)y + (x - 4)y + \ldots + y + (y - 2) + (y - 4) + \ldots + 3 + 1$$

$$n(x, y) = \left(\sum_{i=0}^{\left(\frac{x-1}{2} \right)} (x - 2i) \right) y - y \sum_{i=0}^{\left(\frac{y-1}{2} \right)} (y - 2i)$$

$$n(x, y) = \left(\left(\frac{x + 1}{2} \right)^2 - 1 \right) y + \left(\frac{y + 1}{2} \right)^2$$

$$(4.2)$$

However, the equation above does not take into account the number of different pattern elements, v. The effect of v on $n(x, y)$ is introduced in the following equation:

$$n(x, y) = v \left(\left(\left(\frac{x + 1}{2} \right)^2 - 1 \right) y + \left(\frac{y + 1}{2} \right)^2 \right) \qquad (4.3)$$

To illustrate the effect that higher-dimensional patterns have on the number of neurons required in an HGN implementation, the numbers of neutrons for one- and two-dimensional HGN compositions are plotted as a function of the binary pattern size in Figure 4.4. The two-dimensional composition is limited to patterns with quadratic-value sizes, i.e., $x = y$.

The graph shows that a two-dimensional composition requires significantly fewer neurons than a one-dimensional structure. However, the complexity of the HGN algorithm for higher-dimensional structures is not guaranteed to be equivalent to the one-dimensional composition. Furthermore, for large-scale patterns, the size of the network might be very large. In a high-dimensional representation, the collective size of the bias array might be significant. More discussions on this aspect will be presented in later sections.

4.1.3 HGN Recognition Procedure

There are a number of stages in the HGN pattern recognition procedure, including recognition at every layer within the hierarchical structure. The communication paths within the HGN layers are similar to the simple GN implementation. The HGN communications propagate from the base layer neurons to the top neuron, and consequently, from the top neuron to the base layer neurons.

The HGN communications procedure is as follows. Each neuron in the base layer receives an input pattern from an external entity, which we refer to as the Stimulator and Interpreter (SI) module after Nasution and Khan [3]. Each neuron that receives an input is called an active neuron. Each active neuron in the base layer acknowledges that it is active by sending its *p(column, row)*

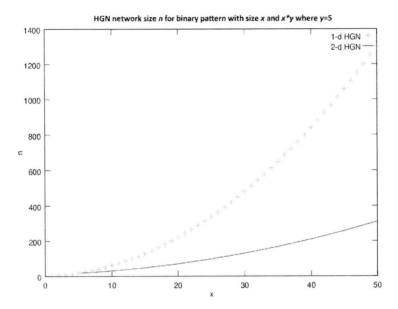

FIGURE 4.4: Total number of neurons in an HGN for one- and two-dimensional compositions as a function of pattern size.

pair to all of the adjacent neurons. For each active neuron in the base layer, the *p(column, row)* pairs received from adjacent neurons make up the bias array entry for the current input pattern. In the end, each non-edge neuron received two pairs from its adjacent neurons; neurons on the edges receive a single pair. Each active neuron must determine its bias index. If the incoming pair combination is found in its bias array, then the index of the entry is noted. Otherwise, a new index is generated to store and reference the pattern. Each active non-edge neuron sends its index to its corresponding neuron in the same column of the higher layer. This process continues until the top layer has been reached. The top layer neuron decides if the input is to be treated as a new pattern and stored or treated as a previously known pattern and recalled. A new index value is propagated downward for a stored pattern, and an existing index value is propagated downward for a recalled pattern.

In the HGN recognition procedure, the bias array structure of the hierarchical composition follows the bias array formation in a GN network. Nevertheless, it has been modified to accommodate the recognition procedures of higher layer neurons based on adjacency comparisons made by lower layer neurons. These are the bias entry conditions for neurons within any HGN network:

1. For neurons in the base layer, their bias entry takes the form {*left, right*}, where *left* and *right* represent the row number of left-adjacent and right-adjacent neurons, respectively.

2. For neurons in the middle layer, their bias entry takes the form {*leftIndex, lowerIndex, rightIndex*}, where *leftIndex, lowerIndex,* and *rightIndex* represent indices obtained from its left, lower (within the same column), and right neurons, respectively.

3. The bias entry structure of the top layer neuron is in the form {*lowerIndex*}, which is the index obtained from its lower layer neuron (within the same column).

4.2 Complexity and Scalability of Hierarchical DPR Scheme

4.2.1 Complexity Estimation

The following discussion focuses on the complexity analysis of the HGN pattern recognition scheme. We will focus on the bias array capacity analysis and Big-O estimation of the HGN network. A similar analysis was carried out on a GN network in Section 3.3.

For Big-O estimation, the HGN strictly follows the adjacency comparison approach of the GN recognition procedure. The difference between the HGN and GN implementations is their execution process. The HGN applies multiple-stage execution (based on the hierarchical structure), and GN implements single-stage execution. Therefore, the Big-O estimation of the complexity of the HGN is $O(n)$.

In the storage capacity analysis, we consider the bias array capacity of each neuron within the HGN composition. A detailed analysis of the HGN storage capacity has been discussed in [3]. Though we do not intend to repeat the explanation in this book, a summary of the complexity estimation will be presented.

In this analysis, the size of the bias array is observed as different patterns are stored. The number of possible pattern combinations increases exponentially with increasing pattern size. The impact of the pattern size on the bias array storage is an important factor in any bias array complexity analysis. The analysis is conducted by segregating the bias arrays according to the layers of a particular HGN network. The following equations show the bias array size estimation for binary patterns. This bias array size is determined using the number of bias entries recorded for each neuron.

4.2.1.1 At the base layer (0):

The size of the bias array for a base layer neuron in an HGN composition strictly follows the estimation given for the GN algorithm. The maximum size of the bias array for each neuron is derived from the number of possible adjacency information combinations (from preceding and succeeding neurons). We consider the number of rows (different pattern elements), n_{row}, for each pattern set used. The maximum bias array size for a non-edge neuron in an HGN for one-dimensional patterns, $\sigma_{(max,ne,0)}$, is given by the following:

$$\sigma_{(max,ne,0)} = n_{row}^2 \tag{4.4}$$

Each neuron at the edge of the layer receives adjacency information only from its preceding or succeeding neuron. Therefore, its maximum bias array size, $\sigma_{(max,e,0)}$, is given by the following:

$$\sigma_{(max,e,0)} = n_{row} \tag{4.5}$$

The maximum bias array size for edge neurons is equivalent to the number of different pattern elements. Consequently, the total size of the bias array for all neurons in the base layer, $\sigma_{(total,0)}$ for patterns of size $S = a$ is derived using an approach similar to that described in Section 3.3:

$$\begin{aligned}
\sigma_{(total,0)} &= n_{row} \left(\sigma_{(max,ne0)} \times (a - 2) + 2\sigma_{(max,e,0)} \right) \\
&= n_{row} \left(n_{row}^2 \times (a - 2) + 2n_{row} \right) \\
&= n_{row}^2 \left(n_{row} \times (a - 2) + 2 \right)
\end{aligned} \tag{4.6}$$

4.2.1.2 At layer i:

In an HGN implementation, neurons in the middle layer receive indices from lower/base layer neurons and perform a recognition procedure using these values. Therefore, the maximum bias array size of neurons at lower/base layer affects the calculation of bias array estimates for the middle layer neurons. The maximum size of the bias array for a non-edge neurons in middle layer i, is derived as follows:

$$\begin{aligned}
\sigma_{(max,ne,i)} &= n_{row}^2 \times \sigma_{(max,ne,i-1)} \\
&= n_{row}^2 \times n_{row}^{2i} \\
&= n_{row}^{2i+2}
\end{aligned} \tag{4.7}$$

Similarly, for edge neurons:

$$\sigma_{(\max,e,i)} = n_{row} \times \sigma_{(\max,e,i-1)}$$
$$= n_{row} \times n_{row}^{2i} \qquad (4.8)$$
$$= n_{row}^{2i+1}$$

The total size of the maximum bias array for all neurons in middle layer i, is determined from the following equation:

$$\sigma_{(total,i)} = n_{row} \left(\sigma_{(\max,ne,i)} \left(a - (2i+2) \right) + 2\sigma_{(\max,e,i)} \right)$$
$$= n_{row} \left(n_{row}^{2i+2} \left(a - (2i+2) \right) + 2n_{row}^{2i+1} \right) \qquad (4.9)$$
$$= n_{row}^{2i+3} \left(n_{row} \left(a - (2i+2) \right) + 2n_{row}^{2i+2} \right)$$

4.2.1.3 Neurons at the top layer:

At the top layer, the maximum size of the bias array is derived from the maximum bias array size of the non-edge neuron in the previous level. Therefore, the maximum size of the bias array at the top level is as follows:

$$\sigma_{(\max,top)} = n_{row} \times \sigma_{(\max,ne,top-1)}$$
$$= n_{row} \times n_{row}^{a-1} \qquad (4.10)$$
$$= n_{row}^{a}$$

The maximum bias array size for the HGN composition, σ_{HGN}, is obtained by summing of all the bias arrays given in the previous equations.

$$\sigma_{HGN} = \sigma_{(total,0)} + \sum_{i=1}^{\left(\frac{a+1}{2}\right)-2} \sigma_{(total,i)} + \sigma_{(\max,top)}$$

$$\sigma_{HGN} = n_{row}^{2} \left(n_{row} \left(a - 2 \right) + 2 \right)$$
$$+ \left(\sum_{i=1}^{\left(\frac{a+1}{2}\right)-2} n_{row}^{2i+3} \left(a - (2i+2) + 2 \right) + 2n_{row}^{2i+2} \right) \qquad (4.11)$$
$$+ n_{row}^{a}$$

To analyze the complexity of an HGN implementation, the maximum bias array size was derived. The results indicate that the size of the bias array is sensitive to the size of the network and the pattern size. However, this result is based on totally unique patterns and does not account for patterns that have similar subpattern features or a close resemblance. In this context, a uniform distribution could be used to estimate the average bias array size for a given pattern set being stored in the network. The average size of the bias array can be determined from the number of stored patterns divided by the maximum number of unique patterns (from combinations of different pattern elements for a given pattern size), i.e., $\frac{n_p}{n_{row}^a}$, where n_p represents the number of patterns stored in the HGN composition.

4.2.2   Scalability in HGN Approach

The HGN pattern recognition scheme is capable of performing highly accurate analyses on patterns using an in-network processing approach. Instead of relying on single-processing (or CPU-centric) recognition schemes, this approach enables collaborations between processing nodes to recognize large-scale patterns. Nevertheless, an increase in the pattern size leads to an overgrown network. As shown in Sections 4.1.2 and 4.2.1, the pattern size has a significant effect on the number of neurons required and the storage capacity of each neuron's bias array.

The number of neurons generated in an HGN implementation has a quadratic dependence on the size of the pattern. Figure 4.5 shows the number of neurons in a one-dimensional HGN recognition scheme for patterns as a function of the number of different elements and the pattern size.

To prevent the overgrowth of the network, Nasution [52] proposed distributing a complex HGN composition across a number of high performance computers. The proposed distribution will be discussed further in the next section.

4.3   Reducing Hierarchical Complexity: A Distributed Approach

As demonstrated in Section 4.1.2, the size of the HGN network grows significantly with increasing pattern size and dimension. For instance, given a binary pattern recognizer with 128-bit pattern representation, the number of neurons required in a one-dimensional HGN implementation is 8450; a two-dimensional implementation with 16×8 representation requires approximately 326 neurons. In applications that have resource-constraint characteristics, such as event detection in wireless sensor networks (WSNs)(WSN), a large number of neurons might not be available. To reduce the effect of the hierarchical structure, a number of approaches have been considered and will be discussed in this book.

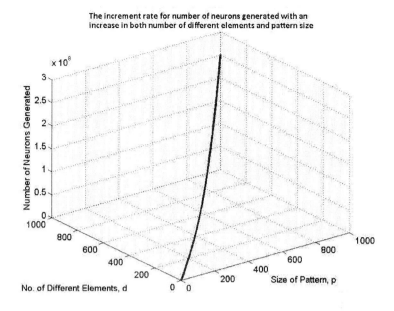

FIGURE 4.5: Growth rate of neurons in an HGN composition as a function of the number of different pattern elements and the pattern size. ©IEEE. Reprinted, with permission, from Amin, A.H.M.; Khan, A.I.; "A divide-and-distribute approach to single-cycle learning HGN network for pattern recognition," 11th International Conference on Control Automation Robotics & Vision (ICARCV), 2010, pp.2118-2123, 7-10 Dec. 2010 doi: 10.1109/ICARCV.2010.5707852.

4.3.1   Distributed Neurons of HGN Network

According to Nasution [52], an HGN network can be decomposed into a number of sub-compositions, according to the number of hosts available in the physical network. Figure 4.6 shows a one-dimensional HGN composition for a pattern of size 13, distributed onto four different hosts. Each neuron in the composition is treated as a memory block on a host that is communicated through an allocated terminal known as a port. In a computer system, a port is used to establish communication channels between processes.

Each neuron in this network model is supplied with an additional parameter known as the port number. The port number identifies each neuron and is used in inter-neuron communications. The communication between hosts is achieved using physical communication, such as the Ethernet (using IP address). Limitations of this approach include the following:

1. Additional parameter and indices. Each neuron in the composition needs to acquire a unique port number, column index, row index, and ID. The

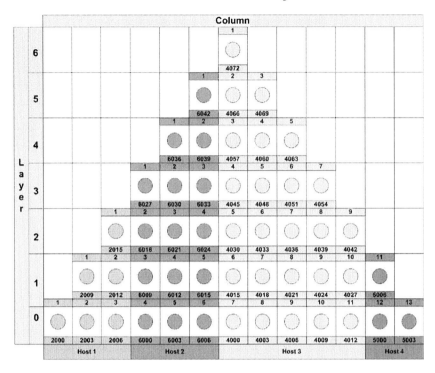

FIGURE 4.6: Decomposition of an HGN onto a number hosts in a physical network.

layer index is also required to indicate the neuron's level in the hierarchy. These additional indices and parameter increase the complexity of the processes involved in the HGN recognition scheme. In addition, these values must be pre-assigned before performing the actual recognition process. Nevertheless, the change in complexity is minimal.

2. The port number assigned to each neuron must be pre-determined. In addition, each neuron must be able to calculate the port number of its adjacent neurons before any communication can occur. This pre-arrangement requires all neurons to evoke an additional pre-processing step to identify and calculate the destination ports of its preceding and succeeding neurons.

3. All of the hosts involved must stay "alive" for the duration of the recognition process. This effect will create high-interdependency between hosts. The recognition process will be prone to a total failure if any single host fails. In addition, the massive and rapid passing of messages between neurons with different port numbers results in a cost of communication between hosts.

With these limitations in mind, a different arrangement of the HGN composition was proposed by Khan and Muhamad Amin [46, 64], that can be distributed across a physical network with low-interdependency between hosts and a low requirement for the number of neurons within its structure. Moreover, changes to the complexity level of the HGN are minimized, thereby retaining its overall structure.

4.3.2 Distributed HGN Approach

This section describes an overview of the distributed HGN scheme. A case study on this approach has been published as a book chapter by Khan et al. [64]. The HGN with distributed approach implements divide-and-distribute techniques by dividing patterns into subpatterns, and delegating these subpatterns to each host available to carry out the recognition procedure using the HGN sub-composition.

The distributed HGN extends the original HGN infrastructure wherein its composition is decomposed into several sub-compositions. The method is different from the previous approach, in which the entire HGN structure was decomposed and delegated to available hosts. The distributed HGN decomposes the HGN network by creating smaller sub-networks, each acting as an actual HGN network that performs recognition on subpatterns. Instead of using the whole patterns as inputs, each pattern is segmented into smaller parts and each of the pattern segments acts as an input to the respective HGN sub-network composition. Figure 4.7 shows the logical illustration of the decomposition of the HGN into HGN sub-compositions.

Each of the HGN subnets has the ability to process pattern segments independently. Therefore, the compositions may be independently mapped onto the available nodes in the network without losing the accuracy of the HGN. Figure 4.8 shows a comparison between the numbers of GNs required for the original HGN formation and our proposed distributed HGN approach. The comparison is based on binary pattern segments of bit-size 7, which corresponds to an overall pattern of 7-bit increments for the HGN. The distributed HGN scheme requires less than 1500 nodes to process a 245-bit binary pattern. The original HGN structure requires approximately 30,000 nodes for a similar recognition process.

An important consideration in the development of this approach was that the distribution of the large HGN network to smaller HGN subnets allowed each subnet to be assigned to a specific host in a physical network. There are two advantages to having a smaller composition on each host:

1. Due to the smaller HGN structure, a smaller capacity of memory space is allocated for each HGN subnet.

2. Maintaining only inter-HGN communications reduces communication costs for inter-neuron communications.

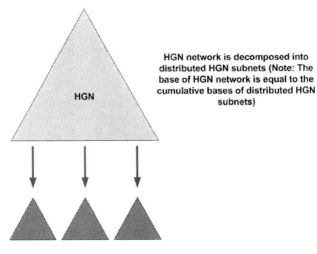

Distributed HGN Subnets

FIGURE 4.7: HGN Decomposition into distributed HGN sub-networks. The HGN network is decomposed into three HGN subnets.

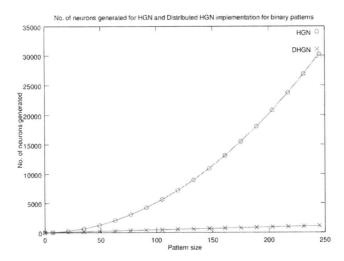

FIGURE 4.8: Comparison of the numbers of GNs required in the HGN and the distributed HGN as a function of pattern size. A 7-bit pattern segment is used for each HGN subnet in the distributed HGN scheme.

Within each host, the HGN subnet is structured as an executable code, and each neuron is represented as an associative data structure in a block of memory space for storing and recalling patterns. The communications between neurons is achieved using either a sequential or parallel processing approach, via a message-passing infrastructure, such as Message Passing Interface (MPI). Each neuron can also be represented as a processing unit in a multi-core processor machine. Different configurations of this distributed HGN scheme will be discussed in the next chapter.

To obtain an overall view of patterns, the distributed HGN scheme allows communications between HGN subnets residing on different hosts. The communications involve message exchanges containing indices obtained from each of the HGN subnets for every subpattern analyzed by the network. Cumulatively, these indices represent the entire pattern structure.

The accuracy and scalability of a distributed approach for the HGN algorithm have been verified using two significant factors related to the deployment of an application on any distributed systems:

1. The varying capabilities of the participating nodes

2. The distribution of the computational load

Two distributed schemes were simulated. The first verification addresses varying processing capabilities within a distributed system through the non-uniform approach. The second demonstrates the distributiveness of the approach through the uniform distributed HGN model. The following section describes the design of this distributed HGN approach by considering these two factors.

4.4 Design Evaluation for Distributed DPR Approach

We consider two different network distribution approaches for distributing the HGN network into different subnets. These approaches are the uniform and non-uniform approaches.

4.4.1 Non-Uniform Distribution

The distributed approach in HGN takes the form of multiple HGN compositions. These compositions are distributed across the network. In the non-uniform model, the compositions may vary in size. For this simulation, a 7-21-7 composition was chosen; there are three sub-structures, comprising two 7-element HGNs, and one 21-element HGN. Figure 4.9 illustrates these compositions. Note that in this diagram, the middle host/network has been determined to be substantially larger than the other two hosts/networks.

FIGURE 4.9: Non-uniform distributed HGN approach with 7-21-7 compositions for 35-element patterns with two possible values. (With kind permission from John Wiley & Sons, Inc.: Mobile Intelligence, "An Online Scheme for Threat Detection Within Mobile Ad Hoc Networks," pp. 380-411, 2010, Khan, A. I. and Muhamad Amin, A. H. and Raja Mahmood, R. A., Figure 17.13, http://dx.doi.org/10.1002/9780470579398.ch17.)

The non-uniform distribution takes the environment into account. Some parts of the network might have lower power resources, and thus their processing capabilities are lower than other parts of the network. With this scenario in mind, the effect of an unbalanced composition on the pattern recognition accuracy of the distributed approach is analyzed.

The results of this simulation show that the non-uniform model offers an almost equivalent level of accuracy to the HGN. Furthermore, it requires less neurons in its composition. The number of neurons required for a single HGN composition can be derived from Equation 4.1. The number of neurons required, $n\left(x_{(all,s)}\right)$ for s subnets in a distributed HGN composition for a pattern of size $S = a$ is determined using the following equation:

$$n\left(x_{(all,s)}\right) = v\left(\left(\frac{a_1+1}{2}\right)^2 + \left(\frac{a_2+1}{2}\right)^2 + \ldots + \left(\frac{a_s+1}{2}\right)^2\right); \ for \ \sum_{i=1}^{s} a_i$$

$$= v\left(\sum_{i=1}^{s}\left(\frac{a_i+1}{2}\right)^2\right) \tag{4.12}$$

Note that the squared term in Equation 4.12 is be substantially smaller than the squared term in Equation 4.1 for the same sized problem, resulting in fewer required neurons.

The mapping process in our simulation begins with the input of the patterns. Each of the patterns, as shown in Table 4.4, are segmented and loaded

TABLE 4.4: Character Representations of 35-bit Patterns Using a Horizontal Scanning Approach

Character	35-bit Representation
A	00100010101000111111100011000110001
I	11111000010000110001100011000101110
J	01111100001000001110000010000111110
S	10001100010101000100010101000110001
X	10001100010101000100010101000110001
Z	11111000010001000100010001000011111

(With kind permission from John Wiley & Sons, Inc.: Mobile Intelligence, "An Online Scheme for Threat Detection Within Mobile Ad Hoc Networks," pp. 380-411, 2010, Khan, A. I. and Muhamad Amin, A. H. and Raja Mahmood, R. A., Table 17.2, http://dx.doi.org/10.1002/9780470579398.ch17.)

```
                                    2
                                1   2   1
                            1   1   2   1   1
                        1   1   1   2   1   1   1
                    2   1   1   1   2   1   1   1   2
                1   2   1   1   1   2   1   1   1   2   1
                2   1   2   1   1   1   2   1   1   1   2   1   2
                1   2   1   2   1   1   1   2   1   1   1   2   1   2   1
        2       2   1   2   1   2   1   1   1   2   1   1   1   2   1   2   1   1                2
    2   1   1   1   2   1   2   1   2   1   1   1   2   1   1   1   2   1   2   1   1        2   1   1
1   2   1   1   2   1   2   1   2   1   2   1   1   1   2   1   1   1   2   1   2   1   1   2   1   2   1   1   1
1   1   2   1   1   2   1   1   2   1   2   1   2   1   1   1   2   1   1   1   2   1   2   1   1   2   1   2   1   1   1   1   2
```

FIGURE 4.10: The HGN subnets successfully store the bitmap pattern for character "*I*" at index 2 after the bit map pattern for character "*A*" was stored in index 1. (With kind permission from John Wiley & Sons, Inc.: Mobile Intelligence, "An Online Scheme for Threat Detection Within Mobile Ad Hoc Networks," pp. 380-411, 2010, Khan, A. I. and Muhamad Amin, A. H. and Raja Mahmood, R. A., Figure 17.14, http://dx.doi.org/10.1002/9780470579398.ch17.)

into the HGN subnets by the SI module. Figure 4.10 shows the bitmap of character "*I*" analyzed by the distributed HGN. Character "*I*" is stored after character "*A*," which has the index value of 1. The results show character "*I*" is a new pattern, which has the index value of 2. For this simulation, each segment was input sequentially. However, in an actual implementation, the processing of these pattern segments will occur in parallel, vastly improving the execution time.

4.4.1.1 Pattern Recognition Process

The overall store or recall decision depends on the decisions reached by the individual HGN subnets. The top-layer neurons of each subnet decide if the subpattern produces a recall or a store. If the pattern segment has not been

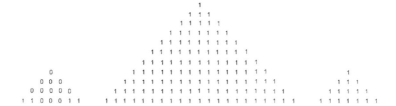

FIGURE 4.11: Results for a 1-bit distortion pattern of character "*A.*" The first HGN subnet shows that a new subpattern has been found (with assigned index 0), whereas other compositions correctly recall this as the pattern associated with index 1 (bitmap pattern of "*A*"). (With kind permission from John Wiley & Sons, Inc.: Mobile Intelligence, "An Online Scheme for Threat Detection Within Mobile Ad Hoc Networks," pp. 380-411, 2010, Khan, A. I. and Muhamad Amin, A. H. and Raja Mahmood, R. A., Figure 17.15, http://dx.doi.org/10.1002/9780470579398.ch17.)

identified, the active top neuron outputs the index value 0. Otherwise, the recalled index of the subpattern will be output. Figure 4.11 shows the result of a 1-bit distorted character pattern "*A*" introduced to the network after the character patterns "*A*," "*I*," "*J*," "*S*," "*X*," and "*Z*" have been stored.

Figure 4.11 shows that only one of the subnets records the subpattern as a new pattern. Other subnets recall the index value of 1, which is the index for the stored character pattern "*A*". The decision of whether the pattern is a recall or store is made based on the cumulative decisions of the distributed HGN subnets using the recall value. Equation 4.13 shows the formula for the recall, R_c of a distributed HGN scheme with s subnets. Note that $n_{(r,i)}$ represents the neurons that produce an index that is similar to the index of the targeted pattern class, r and $n_{(t,i)}$ represents each neuron in subnet i.

$$R_c = \frac{\sum_{i=1}^{s} n_{(r,i)}}{\sum_{i=1}^{s} n(t,i)} \tag{4.13}$$

Using the example from Figure 4.11, the recall value for a 1-bit distortion pattern of character "*A*" is $(4 + 121 + 16) \div (16 + 121 + 16) = 141 \div 153 = 0.9216$. Therefore, its recall percentage is 92.16%.

The distribution of patterns into multiple HGN subnets might improve the recall accuracy of the scheme. According to [64], the recall percentages of 1-bit distorted patterns are significantly higher in the distributed HGN approach than the HGN. This behavior is attributed to the encapsulation effect of the distributed HGN, i.e., the effects of a distortion in a particular subnet do not affect the other subnets. Figure 4.12 shows the encapsulation effect. It also shows the internal state of the subnets from the 1-bit distorted pattern of character "A." The effects of the distortion are limited to the subnet that

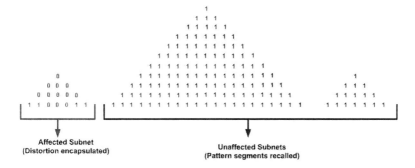

FIGURE 4.12: A 1-bit distortion occurring in the overall input pattern 'A' stays encapsulated within the left composition. (With kind permission from John Wiley & Sons, Inc.: Mobile Intelligence, "An Online Scheme for Threat Detection Within Mobile Ad Hoc Networks," pp. 380-411, 2010, Khan, A. I. and Muhamad Amin, A. H. and Raja Mahmood, R. A., Figure 17.23, http://dx.doi.org/10.1002/9780470579398.ch17.)

analyzed the distorted part of the pattern; the remaining subnets are not affected by the distortion.

The HGN subnets are able to provide higher recall accuracy owing to this encapsulation effect. The downside to this effect is that if the distortion occurs in the larger subnet, the recall accuracy might be adversely affected. This problem can be easily resolved by using compositions of similar size. The uniform approach implements equal-sized compositions.

4.4.2 Uniform Distribution

The uniform model of the distributed HGN is introduced to delimit the effects of distortion location experienced in the non-uniform model. In this pattern recognition simulation, five HGN subnets for 7-bit subpatterns were implemented to analyze 35-bit binary character patterns. Figure 4.13 shows the structure of the compositions.

The uniform approach was developed to enable the distribution of the HGN algorithm for networks comprising small devices and/or limited processing and storage capabilities. With the relatively smaller sized subnets, each processing node/neuron is able to store smaller pattern segments, and thus requires less processing capability for the pattern recognition process. Having similar sized compositions also removes the problem of a single composition affecting the accuracy of the results.

It was reported in [64], that the uniform model's recall values are significantly higher than those of the HGN. The increase in the recall accuracy is owing to the encapsulation effect. The distortions are generally compartmentalized in a specific composition(s), and thus do not affect the findings of

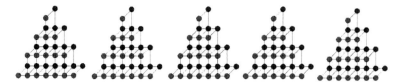

FIGURE 4.13: Uniform distributed model composition for analyzing 35-bit binary patterns. (With kind permission from John Wiley & Sons, Inc.: Mobile Intelligence, "An Online Scheme for Threat Detection Within Mobile Ad Hoc Networks," pp. 380-411, 2010, Khan, A. I. and Muhamad Amin, A. H. and Raja Mahmood, R. A., Figure 17.25, http://dx.doi.org/10.1002/9780470579398.ch17.)

other compositions. The added benefit of the uniform approach is that all the compositions are similar in size, and the problem of an over-sized composition affecting the accuracy of the results is alleviated.

Figure 4.14 shows the encapsulation effect in the uniform distributed approach for character *"A"* with a 2-bit distortion.

This figure indicates that the distorted pattern segments are encapsulated in the first and the third compositions from the left. The rest of the pattern segments are recalled as character *"A"* (represented by the bias index entry of 1).

Generally, the uniform approach produces higher recall accuracy values for distorted patterns than the non-uniform approach. The standard-size encapsulation of the local distortions ensures the better performance of the uniform model of the distributed HGN. A close-up view of the difference in the effects of distortions in the HGN and the uniform approach are illustrated in Figure 4.15. This figure shows the results for a 1-bit distortion using three 7-bit HGN subnets and one 21-bit HGN composition for pattern recognition.

The distortion effect in the HGN composition cannot be localized, and it propagates along the right hand side of the composition (Figure 4.15), leading to a null recall. It is evident that the smaller and similar sized distributed compositions have a better chance of discovering the distorted pattern than a single HGN composition.

In this chapter we have established the fundamental principles of distributed pattern recognition (DPR) schemes. To fulfill the scalability requirements of recognition over large-scale or Internet-scale data, the computational design of these schemes must take into account the size of the network and the neuron capacity. The distributed HGN was chosen as an example to accomplish these requirements. In the next chapter, we will explore the distribution factor, the distributed HGN algorithm, and its capabilities as a distributed pattern recognition algorithm. The distributed HGN (DHGN) as a GN-based algorithm can be considered to be an associative memory (AM) algorithm and has the ability to perform parallel recognition processes.

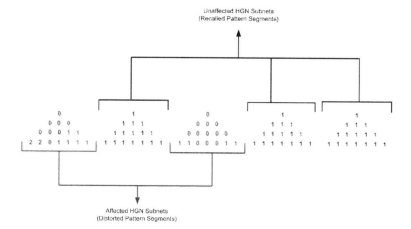

FIGURE 4.14: Encapsulation effect in the uniform model for character "*A*" with a 2-bit distortion. The effects of the distortions are localized in two compositions on the left and do not influence the findings of the remaining compositions. (With kind permission from John Wiley & Sons, Inc.: Mobile Intelligence, "An Online Scheme for Threat Detection Within Mobile Ad Hoc Networks," pp. 380-411, 2010, Khan, A. I. and Muhamad Amin, A. H. and Raja Mahmood, R. A., Figure 17.34, http://dx.doi.org/10.1002/9780470579398.ch17.)

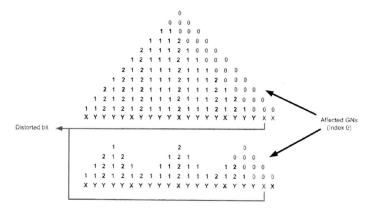

FIGURE 4.15: The effects of a 1-bit distortion in the pattern are localized in the uniformly distributed compositions (lower). The effects of the distorted pattern are propagated along the right side of the HGN composition, leading to a false conclusion. (With kind permission from John Wiley & Sons, Inc.: Mobile Intelligence, "An Online Scheme for Threat Detection Within Mobile Ad Hoc Networks," pp. 380-411, 2010, Khan, A. I. and Muhamad Amin, A. H. and Raja Mahmood, R. A., Figure 17.41, http://dx.doi.org/10.1002/9780470579398.ch17.)

Chapter 5

Recognition via Divide-and-Distribute Approach

As discussed in the previous chapter, the effectiveness of one-shot learning pattern recognition, such as Graph Neuron (GN)–based algorithms can be improved by dividing patterns into subpatterns and distributing them across multiple computational networks. This improvement has a two-fold effect. First, the scalability of the recognition process improves. This approach allows recognition to scale up with the size of patterns and the network capacity to conduct the recognition. Second, the distribution of patterns into subpatterns of equal or different sizes allows for error encapsulation in a particular subnet, and thus recognition is performed more accurately. Nevertheless, the effects of error encapsulation can only be observed when the error is small and concentrated.

Graph Neuron (GN)–based algorithms have been developed based on two different concepts, graph-matching and associative memory. These two concepts give GN-based algorithm implementation the added advantage of scalability. The simple recognition procedure and lightweight algorithm of the GN give it the ability to perform pattern recognition processes on distributed systems. Furthermore, GN algorithms incur low computational and communication costs when deployed in a distributed system. Previous chapters have analyzed both the GN and HGN approaches and introduced a distributed version of the HGN, the Distributed Hierarchical Graph Neuron (DHGN).

5.1 Divide-and-Distribute Approach for One-Shot Learning IS-PR Scheme

An important aspect in the development of pattern recognition schemes is the algorithmic design. A proper design is efficient and has the ability to generate a more accurate classification strategy. In this chapter, the algorithmic design and prospects of using the proposed DHGN algorithm for Internet-scale pattern recognition schemes are extensively discussed. The proposed algorithm extends the scalability of the existing Hierarchical Graph Neuron (HGN) implementation by reducing the computational requirement incurred by the number of neurons required for the recognition processes. The recognition accuracy is comparable to the HGN implementation. In the DHGN, the recognition process can be deployed as a composition of sub-processes that are being executed in parallel across a distributed network. Each sub-process is conducted independently, making it less cohesive than other pattern recognition approaches.

5.1.1 Associative Memory (AM) Concept in Pattern Recognition

From a pattern recognition perspective, AM refers to a set of functions (or a learning network) that has the ability to make an association between input and output. Associative memory, M, as defined in [65], is a system that provides an input-output relationship as follows: $a \rightarrow M \rightarrow b$ where a and b are the input and output, respectively. From this perspective, each input vector is associated with an output vector. The association can be represented as a fundamental set of associations: $\{(a^\mu, b^\mu) \mid \mu = 1, 2, \ldots, p\}$. This set is *a priori* knowledge that must be known by the AM system.

There are two types of AM for pattern recognition, namely auto-associative memory (auto-AM) and hetero-associative memory (hetero-AM). In auto-AM, the system recognizes an input pattern and produces its associated output pattern. Therefore, for a given set of associations, (a^μ, b^μ), the auto-AM rule is true under the following condition: $a^\mu = b^\mu, \forall \mu \in \{1, 2, \ldots, p\}$. Auto-AM enables the system (either neural network or learning system) to pass input patterns through as output patterns without any changes, due to input patterns and output patterns having similar characteristics. The Hopfield network is an example of an auto-AM algorithm.

Alternatively, hetero-AM pattern recognition follows the rule of association; incomplete input patterns can lead to complete output patterns. Therefore, in terms of the association set, (a^μ, b^μ), when $a^\mu \neq b^\mu$, the following rule applies: for $\exists \mu \in \{1, 2, \ldots, p\}$. In this case, given distorted pattern $\bar{a}^x$ of original pattern a^x, the hetero-AM system will be able to gain full recall of pattern a^x. Bidirectional associative memory (BAM) is a neural network approach that adopts the hetero-AM concept. Hetero-AM also offers the ability to conduct a recognition based on patterns of different sizes, such as demonstrated in the work of Kosko [66].

Associative Memory approaches, such as the Hopfield network and Fuzzy Associative Memory (FAM) [67], tend to be computationally intensive and iterative. In contrast, Morphological Associative Memory (MAM) [68] provides a solution within a single iteration, and thus implements single-cycle learning. However, MAM is a tightly coupled scheme, which relies on global maximum/minimum computations and is not readily distributed.

Graph Neuron (GN) based algorithms, including the HGN and DHGN, implement an auto-associative memory approach in their recognition procedure. GN has the ability to recall patterns that have been memorized by the network. The memorization can occur in the pre-execution stage or instantaneously during the recognition process. The former means that the GN algorithm performs a supervised recognition; the latter represents an unsupervised mechanism. Furthermore, GN algorithms perform recognition on patterns of equivalent size. Therefore, the features of auto-AM have been fulfilled.

The scalability of the DHGN and other GN-based algorithms is owing to the adoption of an associative memory approach. The DHGN is an associative memory system that is capable of recognizing patterns (either original or noisy), and it is able to match multiple streams of input with historical data in the network in real-time [61]. For a given pattern, the DHGN also performs an internal association, in the sense that an association between elements of a pattern is considered. For example, given a pattern, P, comprising five elements, $\{p_1, p_2, p_3, p_4, p_5\}$, the DHGN also takes into account the associations set $\{(p_1, p_2), (p_2, p_3), (p_3, p_4), (p_4, p_5)\}$. The following subsection will further discuss the architecture of the DHGN in line with its pattern recognition process.

5.1.2 DHGN Computational Design

The DHGN formalizes the distributed HGN scheme described in Chapter 4. By dividing and distributing subpatterns, the DHGN adds a clustering mechanism for pattern recognition. Each of the subpatterns undergoes a one-shot recognition procedure. The results of the sub-recognition add cumulatively to obtain the actual recognition result.

The DHGN network constitutes a number of DHGN subnets (HGN subcomposition) and a Stimulator/Interpreter Module (SI module) node, as described in Muhamad Amin and Khan [4]. Figure 5.1 shows the complete architecture of the DHGN network. In this figure, the decomposition of binary image pattern *"K"* into subpatterns is illustrated. This decomposition is performed by the SI module node. The input activates the GN nodes that correspond to the bits of the input pattern. In doing so, each pattern element of a subpattern is mapped to the relevant GNs in the respective subnet. Each subnet integrates its responses and sends the results to the SI module to form an overall response.

Communications within the DHGN network occur in a single-cycle environment, i.e., each pattern is passed through the network only once. Recognition result is produced in the form of recall (pattern is known) or store (pattern is memorized). Within each DHGN subnet, the communication between GNs occurs once for each subpattern. By eliminating the need for an iterative mechanism to recall or store patterns, the DHGN offers a fast recognition procedure.

Each DHGN subnet is derived from a composition of inter-connected GNs. The size of the subnet depends on the size of the subpattern and the number of different elements in the subpattern. Therefore, to define the size of each

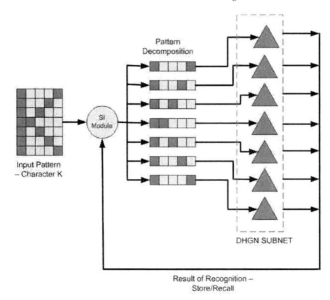

FIGURE 5.1: Pattern recognition processes using DHGN algorithm where a 7 x 5 bitmap of letter K is mapped as subpatterns over 7 hierarchically formed GN sub-networks. (With kind permission from Springer Science+Business Media: AI 2008: Advances in Artificial Intelligence, "Single-Cycle Image Recognition Using an Adaptive Granularity Associative Memory Network", LNCS, 2008, 386-392, Muhamad Amin, A.H., and Khan, A.I., Fig.1, W. Wobcke and M. Zhang (Eds.), http://dx.doi.org/10.1007/978-3-540-89378-3_39.)

subnet, we consider the number of neurons, n_{gn}, required for a subpattern of size s_{sp} composed of v different element given by the following equation:

$$n_{gn} = v \left(\frac{s_{sp} + 1}{2} \right)^2 \tag{5.1}$$

5.1.2.1   Network Generation

In order for the DHGN scheme to perform recognition on patterns, it must first be generated. Network generation involves the construction of SI module node and a collection of DHGN subnets. SI module node is a control node, responsible for managing the inputs and outputs among the DHGN subnets. The distribution of DHGN subnets within the network depends on the pattern decomposition by the SI module. Given a pattern vector $P = \{p_1, p_2, p_3, \ldots, p_m\}$ of size m, and subpattern length s_{sp}. The number of DHGN subnets n_{sn} that needs to be generated is determined by Equation 5.2:

$$n_{sn} = \frac{m}{s_{sp}}, \ s_{sp} \leq m \qquad (5.2)$$

The neurons within a DHGN subnet are structured in hierarchical manner, similar to the HGN. Each layer within the DHGN subnet is populated with neurons. The number of layers, l_{gn}, required within a DHGN subnet is given by the following equation:

$$l_{gn} = \frac{s_{sp} + 1}{2} \qquad (5.3)$$

Note that the number of neuron layers could be directly determined from the calculation of size of the network as shown in Equation 5.1. The conditions for GN node generation within a particular layer are as follows:

1. At base layer l_0, the number of neurons generated $n_{gn}^{l_0}$ is equivalent to the size of subpattern multiplied by the number of different elements v, i.e., $n_{gn}^{l_0} = s_{sp} \times v$.

2. At a middle layer l_i, the number of neurons $n_{gn}^{l_i}$ varies according to the level of the layer i in the hierarchy, except for the top layer. Therefore, $n_{gn}^{l_i} = v \, (s_{sp} - 2i)$.

3. At the top layer l_t, the number of processing neurons required is equivalent to the number of different elements v. Hence, $n_{gn}^{l_t} = v$.

In the network generation stage, SI module is also responsible for initializing DHGN subnets. The initialization involves communication of possible input values to the base layer neurons before the actual store/recall operations can start. The message communication between SI module and base layer neurons (within each DHGN subnets) is conducted using a specific message communication protocol that has been developed for bitmap patterns. SI module sends the possible input values to each DHGN subnet using the *instruction, message* format. For example, if binary values are to be communicated then the message would be *initialize, (0,1)*.

Each initialization message received by the base layer neurons is used for coordination within the base layer. Each neuron represents a specific position. The following pseudo code shows the formation of the base layer neurons for binary pattern recognition:

Note that the initialization process involves uploading distinct *(value, position)* pairs into the respective neurons for later use in the store/recall operations.

Algorithm 2 Base Layer Neuron Formation

1: **for** $n_{gn} \in l_0$ **do**
2:     **if** $GN_{id} \leq s_{sp}$ **then**
3:         $n_{gn,val} = 1$
4:     **else**
5:         $n_{gn,val} = 0$
6:     **end if**
7: **end for**

5.1.2.2 Neuron Communications

Communications in the DHGN recognition scheme involve a message-passing mechanism to allow communication between processing nodes using exchange messages. The mechanism consists of two different types of communication, namely macro- and micro-communication. In macro-communication, communication costs at system level are taken into account, i.e., communications incurred between the SI module and DHGN subnets. Micro-communication is responsible for the communication between neurons in a particular subnet for each pattern introduced into the system.

Macro-communication in DHGN implementations occurs between the SI module node and either the base or top layer of neurons in each subnet. It occurs at three different phases:

1. *Network generation phase:* The SI module is responsible for communicating possible input values of the pattern, which are used in the recognition process, to all base layer neurons in the DHGN subnets. Equation 5.4 shows the number of messages communicated by the SI module to these neurons, $n_{msg}(SI \to sn)$:

$$n_{msg}(SI \to sn) = n_{sn} \times s_{sp} \times v \qquad (5.4)$$

   In this equation, n_{sn} represents the number of available subnets. This equation is based on the assumption that all DHGN subnets are of the same size. The messages communicated from the SI module to each neuron are in the *instruction, message* format, as described earlier.

2. *Pattern input phase:* After all DHGN subnets have been generated, the SI module will perform a divide-and-distribute process on the input pattern. This process decomposes the pattern into a number of subpatterns, based on the number of subnets available. Consequently, these subpatterns are sent to each subnet in the network. However, in the actual implementation, the SI module will communicate directly with each neuron in the base layer of each DHGN subnet. Therefore, the number of messages communicated is similar to the number of messages communicated in the network generation phase (Equation 5.4).

3. *Result communication phase:* After the recognition process in each DHGN subnet is completed, the results (in terms of recall or store) are communicated back to the SI module for further analysis. In this communication, messages comprising the subnet id (sn_{id}), status (sn_{st}), and index stored/recall (sn_{idx}), in the form of sn_{id}, sn_{st}, sn_{idx} are sent to the SI module by all of the top-layer neurons in each subnet. The total number of messages communicated from the subnets to the SI module, n_{msg} $(sn \rightarrow SI)$, is equivalent to the number of subnets available, n_{sn}. Therefore, n_{msg} $(sn \rightarrow SI) = n_{sn}$.

The following relations describe the micro-communications between neurons in each DHGN subnet.

5.1.2.2.1 Base layer For each neuron in the base layer, the number of message communications can be derived from the number of messages communicated between adjacent neurons for each input subpattern. For neurons at the edge of the base layer, the number of communication exchanges is equivalent to the number of different elements in the subpattern. Non-edge neurons communicate with adjacent neurons in both the preceding and the succeeding columns and communicate bias indices to the neurons at the next higher layer. The amount of message exchange is $v^2 + 1$, where v is the number of possible element values. The cumulative communication costs for each input recognition process for all neurons in the base layer of a single DHGN subnet is derived from the following equation:

$$n_{msg}^{l_0} = \left((v^2 + 1) \times (s_{sp} - 2) + 2v \right) \tag{5.5}$$

5.1.2.2.2 Middle layers The communication costs for neurons in the middle layers are similar to that of the base layer. However, the number of neurons available differs for each layer. For each middle layer i, where $1 \leq i \leq l_t$, the number of message exchanges for a single input subpattern recognition is derived as follows:

$$n_{msg}^{l_i} = \left((v^2 + 1) \times (s_{sp} - (2i + 2)) + 2v \right) \tag{5.6}$$

Equation 5.7 presents the cumulative communication costs for all neurons in the middle layers:

$$n_{msg}^{l_{(i,total)}} = \sum_{i=1}^{l_t - 1} \left((v^2 + 1) \times (s_{sp} - (2i + 2)) + 2v \right) \tag{5.7}$$

5.1.2.2.3   Top layer   These neurons are only responsible for communicating the final index for each subpattern stored/recalled to the SI module. The costs for communicating these indices were included in the macrocommunication evaluation.

This subsection has presented a detailed description of the DHGN architecture for distributed pattern recognition. This architecture represents an abstract formation of the network. In reality, this architecture can be deployed in a coarsely distributed or finely distributed network environment.

5.1.3   Dual-Phase Recognition Procedure

The DHGN architecture that has been described in the previous subsection comprises two important entities: the SI module and the DHGN subnets. Recognition of patterns mainly occurs within each DHGN subnet. However, at this instant, all each subnet knows is a sub-composition of the overall pattern. The DHGN system must restructure the overall information of the pattern and produce a result for the entire pattern, i.e., whether the input pattern is known to the system or not. Another phase of recognition is required that involves the results of the recognition processes executed by the subnets.

The recognition procedure for the DHGN implementation can be analogically represented as a distributed analysis procedure, as shown in Figure 5.2. Imagine there is a large block of data that needs to be analyzed. Given a set of analysts, this large block of data can be decomposed into sub-structures of data, and each analyst would work on a sub-structure. In the end, the results of the analysis must be recompiled to form an overall result for the analysis of the large block of data.

The DHGN distributed pattern recognition performs pattern analysis in two phases:

1. Subpattern recognition

2. Pattern reconstruction and recognition

Note that these two phases occur consequently and within a single-cycle recognition mechanism.

5.1.3.1   Phase 1: Subpattern Recognition

In the DHGN implementation, the core recognition process is conducted at the subpattern level. There are four stages involved in this process.

Stage 1.   After receiving an input from the SI module, each activated neuron in the base layer will send a signal message to the nodes in the adjacent columns containing the row number/address of the activated neuron. The activated neurons on the edges of the layer will only send the activation signal message to the neurons in the penultimate columns. The activated neurons that receive the signal

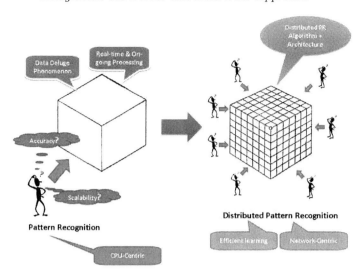

FIGURE 5.2: Analogical representation of the DHGN distributed pattern recognition scheme.

messages from their adjacent neighbors will respond by updating their bias array, noting the activation signals. All other neurons will remain inactive.

Stage 2. All active neurons in the base layer will update their bias arrays. If the bias entry value, σ_{ent} (*left, right*) received from the activated neurons in both the preceding and succeeding columns have been recorded, the index of the entry is sent to the respective neuron in the same position at the higher layer. If the σ_{ent} (*left, right*) value is not found within the bias array, a new index will be created and sent to the neuron in the higher layer. Note that active neurons at the edges of the base layer do not communicate with higher layer neurons. Because of the pyramid-like structure of the DHGN subnets, there are no neurons present at the edges of a higher layer.

Stage 3. The DHGN neurons in the layer above the base that receives a signal message, containing the index of the bias entry that has been created or recalled from stage 2, will be activated. A process similar to stages 1 and 2 will occur. However, the contents of the signal messages from preceding and succeeding columns will be in the form σ_{ent} (*left, middle, right*) for non-edge neurons and either σ_{ent} (*left, middle*) or σ_{ent} (*middle, right*) for the edge neurons. The values for left, middle, and right are derived from the indices retrieved from the lower layer neurons. For instance, left is for the preceding neuron's index received from its lower layer counterpart. After the message communication between adjacent neurons is completed, the active neurons will update their bias arrays and send the stored/recalled index/indices to the neuron at the same position in the higher layer (except for the neurons at the edges). This stage will be repeated for each layer above the base layer, until the top layer neurons are reached.

Stage 4. One of the top layer neurons will receive a bias index from a neuron in the layer underneath. This top layer activated neuron node will search its bias array for the index. If the index is found, this node will trigger a recall flag with the recalled index. Otherwise, it will trigger a store flag and store the new index in its bias array. It will send a signal message to the SI module with the message format $\{sn_{id}, sn_{st}, sn_{idx}\}$, where status is either recall or store. The signal message sent by the top layer active neuron marks the completion of the recognition procedure at the subpattern level. In a DHGN implementation, the lower bias arrays are updated when a new entry is found. Note that the bias index for lower layer neurons might not be the same for a given pattern index.

Figure 5.3 shows the process workflow of the proposed recognition algorithm.

5.1.3.2   Phase 2: Pattern Reconstruction and Recognition

Recognition results obtained by the SI module from all subnets in a DHGN network require further analysis to derive an overall recall of the respective input subpattern. Two methods have been considered. These are recall-percentage and voting methods. These methods differ in terms of the mechanism adopted. This research intends to compare and contrast these two approaches from an accuracy perspective.

5.1.3.2.1   Recall-percentage method   The recall-percentage method underlines the use of bias indices obtained from all neurons in each subnet. The main principle of this approach is that the recall/store decision is based on the cumulative decisions of all neurons in the network.

This method requires that an additional procedure be conducted by each DHGN subnet for the purposes of index collection before final recognition results are submitted to the SI module. For each subpattern introduced into the subnet and after all of the recognition processes have been completed, the activated top neuron will collect all of the index information (idx) from all of the neurons underneath it. These indices are be compiled and structured with the format $\{idx, count\}$. These outputs are sent to the SI module using the message format $\{sn_{id}; (idx_1 : count_1), (idx_2 : count_1), (idx_3 : count_1), \ldots, (idx_n : count_n)\}$ for all n indices recalled or stored.

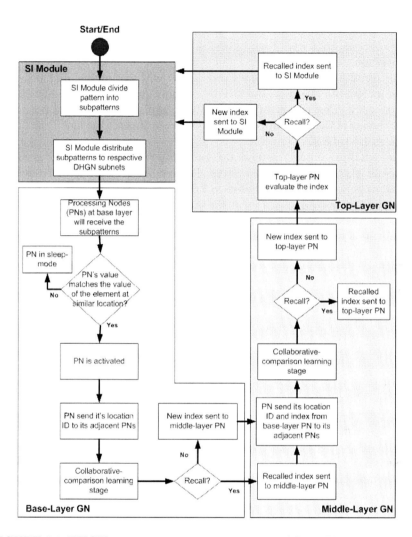

FIGURE 5.3: DHGN pattern recognition process workflow. This diagram represents a DHGN network with three-layer subnets. (With kind permission from Springer Science+Business Media: Neural Process. Lett., "Distributed Multi-Feature Recognition Scheme for Greyscale Images," vol.33, issue 1, pp. 45-59, (February 2011), Muhamad Amin, A.H., and Khan, A.I., Fig.3, http://dx.doi.org/10.1007/s11063-010-9163-8.)

An advantage of the recall-percentage implementation for recognition at the pattern level is the high recall value precision, in terms of the percentages of pattern indices being recalled. For a given input pattern, the DHGN is able to provide a precise recall value. The DHGN also has the ability to use previous input patterns that have been stored in the network to analyze the pattern composition.

The recall-percentage method also comes with a number of limitations. These include its effect on the DHGN recognition accuracy, as described in Section 4.3.2. The nature of the DHGN recognition process implies that a slight change in the structure of the subpattern will affect the index calculation of the entire subnet.

The recall-percentage method also raises issues regarding the level of confidence in the outputs of the system. For instance, assuming a recognition output of a pattern obtained from a DHGN network consists of three patterns previously stored — $P_1 : 0.4$; $P_2 : 0.3$; $P_3 : 0.3$; — the result of this recognition will favor P_1 as the recalled pattern. However, criteria of P_2 and P_3 have also been detected in the pattern. Therefore, there is a need to establish a level of confidence for this type of result from the perspective of recognition.

5.1.3.2.2 Voting method Most of the existing pattern recognition schemes apply rejection techniques to remove highly distorted patterns from its classification procedure. This technique adopts the rejection/accuracy rate as a parameter to indicate levels of similarity between patterns. The technique offers a precise means to obtain a good classification measurement. However, it is most suitable for deployment in a single-decision system, i.e., the classification is conducted using a single classifier/recognizer. A decision-making mechanism is needed to combine all of the decisions (in terms of accuracy/rejection) made by each of the classifiers.

One possible method for combining decisions on classification is the voting method. There are several forms of voting available in the literature. These include majority, common-consent, unison, and unanimity voting [69, 70]. In a DHGN implementation, majority voting is used as a means to obtain a combined decision on the recalls made by each of the subnets within a recognition network.

For each recognition process, whether the input pattern has been recognized (i.e., recall) or is new to the network (i.e., store) is decided by obtaining the majority consent from all of the DHGN subnets. For a pattern to be recalled, the network should confirm that most of the subpatterns belong to the respective input pattern. The adopted majority voting concept follows the work by Cruz, Sossa and Barrón [71] and is described in [4].

In this pattern reconstruction and recognition process, the SI module will initially receive all of the results from the recognition at the subpattern level in the form of signal messages from the DHGN subnets. After all of these

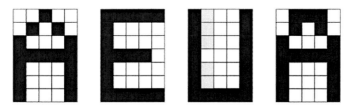

FIGURE 5.4: Samples of binary character images.

messages are received, the actual recognition process is carried out. There are two stages involved at this level.

1. All of the indices received from the DHGN subnets for original patterns are stored in a two-dimensional vector matrix, $S = \{s_{11}, s_{12}, \ldots, s_{mn}\}$. The width of the matrix is equivalent to the size of the pattern, i.e., m; the height corresponds to the number of stored patterns, n.

2. The frequency of the indices is calculated for each test pattern. All of the indices for the test pattern are stored in a vector, $R = \{r_1, r_2, \ldots, r_m\}$. The width of the matrix is equivalent to the size of the pattern. If an entry in vector R gives the list of indices as $\{1, 2, 2, 2, 1\}$, this indicates that three subnets have given a recall result of pattern 2; two subnets have given a recall result of pattern 1. Therefore, based on the voting approach, the pattern will be recalled as pattern 2.

To describe the voting mechanism, a simple pattern recognition problem follows. Figure 5.4 shows four binary character images: A, E, U, and a distorted version of A.

The binary patterns for characters A, E, U, and the distorted image A, P_A, P_E, P_U, and $P_{\bar{A}}$ are shown below:

$$P_A = \begin{pmatrix} 0 & 0 & 1 & 0 & 0 \\ 0 & 1 & 0 & 1 & 0 \\ 1 & 0 & 0 & 0 & 1 \\ 1 & 1 & 1 & 1 & 1 \\ 1 & 0 & 0 & 0 & 1 \\ 1 & 0 & 0 & 0 & 1 \\ 1 & 0 & 0 & 0 & 1 \end{pmatrix} P_E = \begin{pmatrix} 1 & 1 & 1 & 1 & 1 \\ 1 & 0 & 0 & 0 & 0 \\ 1 & 0 & 0 & 0 & 0 \\ 1 & 1 & 1 & 1 & 0 \\ 1 & 0 & 0 & 0 & 0 \\ 1 & 0 & 0 & 0 & 0 \\ 1 & 1 & 1 & 1 & 1 \end{pmatrix}$$

$$P_U = \begin{pmatrix} 1 & 0 & 0 & 0 & 1 \\ 1 & 0 & 0 & 0 & 1 \\ 1 & 0 & 0 & 0 & 1 \\ 1 & 0 & 0 & 0 & 1 \\ 1 & 0 & 0 & 0 & 1 \\ 1 & 0 & 0 & 0 & 1 \\ 1 & 1 & 1 & 1 & 1 \end{pmatrix} P_{\bar{A}} = \begin{pmatrix} 0 & 1 & 1 & 1 & 0 \\ 0 & 1 & 0 & 1 & 0 \\ 1 & 0 & 0 & 0 & 1 \\ 1 & 1 & 1 & 1 & 1 \\ 1 & 0 & 0 & 0 & 1 \\ 1 & 0 & 0 & 0 & 1 \\ 1 & 0 & 0 & 0 & 1 \end{pmatrix}$$

TABLE 5.1: Recalled Indices Retrieved from the DHGN Subnets after Each Pattern Input

		DHGN Subnets						
		k_1	k_2	k_3	k_4	k_5	k_6	k_7
Patterns	P_A	1	1	1	1	1	1	1
	P_E	2	2	2	2	2	2	2
	P_U	3	3	3	3	1	1	2
	P_A^d	4	1	1	1	1	1	1

Each pattern is decomposed into subpatterns and is sent to the DHGN subnets for the first level recognition process. In this example, each character pattern is decomposed into seven subpatterns; each subpattern represents a row of binary values, as shown below:

$$P_A = \begin{pmatrix} 0\,0\,1\,0\,0 \\ 0\,1\,0\,1\,0 \\ 1\,0\,0\,0\,1 \\ 1\,1\,1\,1\,1 \\ 1\,0\,0\,0\,1 \\ 1\,0\,0\,0\,1 \\ 1\,0\,0\,0\,1 \end{pmatrix} \rightarrow \begin{matrix} P_A^1 = (00100) \\ P_A^2 = (01010) \\ P_A^3 = (10001) \\ P_A^4 = (11111) \\ P_A^5 = (10001) \\ P_A^6 = (10001) \\ P_A^7 = (10001) \end{matrix}$$

The results of the recognition process from the subpattern level are sent back to the SI module node. These results, in the form of recalled/new indices for each subnet, sn, are received by the SI module node and are represented by a voting matrix, V, shown in Table 5.1.

The results of the recognition processes show that when the character pattern A is introduced, all subnets respond with index 1. This shows that all subnets agree that this is a newly stored pattern. Similarly, when pattern E is being introduced, all subnets give feedback with an increase in the index value, i.e., index 2. Consequently, pattern U obtains various results from the DHGN subnets. Four out of seven subnets produce a new index, two subnets recall the index of pattern A, and one gave the index of pattern E. In this case, the maximum number of recalled/new indices is chosen as the recalled/new pattern. Similarly, for the distorted pattern A, the index recalled most often is index 1, which correlates with pattern A. Therefore, pattern A is recalled.

Consider that P is an array of stored patterns, $P = \{p_1, p_2, p_3, \ldots, p_m\}$, where m represents the number of patterns being stored. For any pattern p_x to be recalled, the maximum vote $V_{\max}^{p_x}$, is obtained using the following equation:

$$V_{\max}^{p_x} = \arg \max (w_x), \qquad\qquad x \in m \qquad\qquad (5.8)$$

where w_x represents the voting element of pattern p_x in the voting vector W_P. Note that the recognition process for each pattern occurs in a single-cycle containing a fixed number of steps. Additionally, the DHGN can adopt an unsupervised learning approach, which requires no prior training on pattern data.

5.2 Dimensionality Reduction in Pattern Pre-Processing

Pre-processing is an important task carried out before any recognition procedure. To ensure that pattern data are in the specific form required by the algorithm or implementation, pre-processing is a pre-requisite for some pattern recognition systems. Moreover, to ensure that the data are well-distributed and do not contain any outlier values, raw pattern data might need to be normalized before recognition.

Complex data, such as images, environmental sensory readings, and biomedical and biochemical structural data, are usually of high dimensions (more than one). There are two approaches that can be used to reduce the dimensional complexity of data:

1. *Structural reduction*: In this approach, the structure of the data is reduced to a lower dimension.

2. *Content reduction*: In this approach, high dimension data are reduced to an equivalent low-dimension form using a data dimensionality reduction technique.

In this section, these two approaches are discussed in relation to a DHGN implementation.

5.2.1 Structural Reduction

Structural reduction in DHGN pre-processing reduces the structural composition of patterns from high-dimensional structure to its corresponding low-dimensional representation. In this approach, pattern data undergoes structural deformation, but the contents or elements within the pattern remain intact. Structural reduction works on the premise that the structure of data is unlikely to be play a significant role in determining the characteristics of the pattern.

Consider two-dimensional binary images of size 7-by-5 bits, i.e., 35-bit images, as shown in Figure 5.5. In the structural reduction approach, images are rearranged into a one-dimensional bit-string. This rearrangement enables the algorithm to work on patterns in a low structural dimension. From the perspective of a DHGN implementation, this approach enables each subnet to

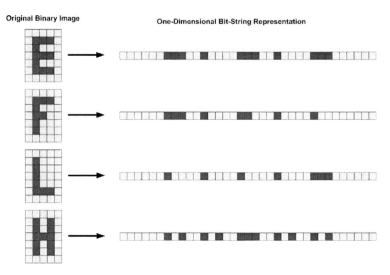

FIGURE 5.5: Structural reduction on binary character images into one-dimensional bit-string representation.

conduct the recognition process using a simple one-dimensional DHGN subnet structure. Therefore, it reduces the structural complexity of the DHGN subnets in the network. An advantage of using this structural reduction approach is that it reduces the structural complexity of patterns while maintaining the integrity of the contents or elements of the patterns. Thus, the content information in each pattern is preserved.

A limitation of this approach is the loss of structural information related to the pattern. The structure of the pattern or data is unknown to the system. Consider the images in Figure 5.5. The DHGN pattern recognizer does not know that the image represents a character *"E."* Rather, it acknowledges the bit information and its association between neighboring pixels in a one-dimensional formation.

5.2.2 Content Reduction

In content reduction, more generally known as the dimensionality reduction approach, features are selected or extracted from the data and are used in the pattern recognition system. It also transforms the data from a high-dimensional space to its equivalent low dimension format. Examples of dimensionality reduction techniques include Principal Components Analysis (PCA), the Linear Discriminant Analysis (LDA), Local Linear Embedding (LLE), and Kohonen maps.

The dimensionality reduction approach allows the recognition system to obtain the best and most cost-efficient data representation of the original raw data obtained from sensory devices or the surroundings. However, some dimensionality reduction techniques require expensive computations for feature processing, selection, and extraction.

There are other techniques that have been proposed for dimensionality reduction that incur a low-level of computational complexity. For instance, in content-based image retrieval (CBIR), histograms and signatures are commonly used for dimensionality reduction for images retrieved using color features [72].

5.3   Remarks on DHGN DPR Scheme

This chapter has presented the Distributed Hierarchical Graph Neuron (DHGN), an approach proposed for distributed pattern recognition. The DHGN implements a divide-and-distribute technique for the HGN networks. The single-cycle learning and in-network processing features of GN-based algorithms in the DHGN lead to an efficient recognition scheme that has high recall accuracy [4]. Furthermore, because of its ability to distribute the recognition process across a computational network, the recognition times of the DHGN's distributed pattern recognition scheme are low and stable. The DHGN is able to lower the storage capacity and communication complexities of the pattern recognition process. In addition, the two-level recognition implemented in the DHGN algorithm offers recognition at both the pattern and subpattern levels, which contributes to the higher recall accuracy for simple and complex data. Moreover, the use of dimensionality reduction schemes, such as binary signature, implies low computational requirements for a DHGN deployment. The extensive works on the DHGN DPR scheme for image and optical character (OCR) recognition can be reviewed in [4, 46, 73]. Note that the DHGN scheme discussed in this chapter were being considered for complex data that have multiple data values and dimensions. This consideration will be further discussed in Part IV of this book.

Part III

Systems and Tools

Chapter 6

Internet-Scale Applications Development

Since the advent of Internet and World Wide Web (WWW) technologies in the mid-1990s, we have witnessed the explosive growth of distributed applications ranging from business applications, such as e-commerce, financial services, and healthcare, to engineering and scientific applications, such as industrial automation, event detection, and biomedical diagnosis. There are two forces driving this growth: the availability of multiple distributed system models and the development of different types of parallel programming techniques. The availability of several distributed models enables system developers to consider the best approach to address requirements specific to a user. Parallel programming techniques allow developers to customize the parallelization scheme to address a specific problem and to a develop system or application software that is deployable and scalable with the expansion of data. Significant attention should be paid to the distributed system models and programming techniques used to develop Internet-scale pattern recognition schemes in distributed applications. These aspects ensure the scalability and efficiency of the recognition schemes when processing large-scale and complex data.

In this chapter, we will discuss the two forces driving the expansion of distributed applications for Internet-scale environments. We will present examples of distributed models and parallel programming techniques that are commonly used in distributed applications development.

6.1 Distributed Computing Models for IS-PR

In this section, a number of existing distributed computing models will be presented. These include the commodity grid, cloud computing, and peer-to-peer (P2P) computing. These distributed models are extensions of conventional distributed system models, such as the client-server and processor-pool models, and were developed to provide a more scalable approach for complex and large-scale computational applications.

6.1.1 Commodity Grid (CoG)

The evolution of grid computing has led to the development of grid software, which coordinates the requirements of the grid environment. Software for the grid must address various issues, such as virtualization, security, resource, data and information management. Commodity-Grid Middleware provides end-users the ability to access and process information across the grid environment. Commodity Grid is derived from the merger of commodity computing and grid computing technologies. Distributed computing technologies, such as JINI, CORBA, and DCOM, originated from commodity computing. The integration of commodity and grid service technologies aims to enhance the functionality, maintenance, and deployment of grid services. The Commodity Grid (CoG) Project [74] is an initiative to develop commodity-grid services. CoG offers an end-to-end solution for grid workflow management. It also provides the architecture for grid-enablement of different types of applications.

6.1.1.1 Java CoG Kit

The Java CoG Kit is a tool for developing a grid workflow management system. It was derived from the CoG Project. The CoG Kit provides end-users an abstraction of the services provided by a grid system. The end-users are not required to know the underlying processes of the system. Their only requirement is to input data into the grid and receive the outputs. The Java CoG Kit provides process abstraction and workflow management using a layered approach. Figure 6.1 shows the layered approach of the Java CoG Kit adopted from [75].

Note that there are a number of services underneath the layered architecture that can be accessed by the end-users. In addition, the Java CoG Kit allows the integration of several grid middleware products. The Java Cog Kit provides abstractions for some processes, such job execution, file transfer, workflow abstraction, and job queuing. The Java CoG Kit introduces the concept of Gridfaces. Gridfaces offer abstractions with respect to the locality of the services provided in the grid. For instance, a grid end-user may browse a remote grid directory to locate a stand-alone application or grid portal.

6.1.2 Cloud Computing

Cloud computing is a new computing paradigm. In business perspective, it allows users to tap into tremendous computing resources on pay-per-use basis without any needs to invest in new infrastructure, training new personnel, or licensing new software. In scientific computing perspective, cloud eventually derived from grid computing paradigm in which a collaboration of computing resources being made available for users, similar to the analogy of power grid made available to each household.

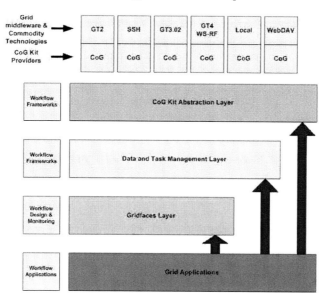

FIGURE 6.1: Java CoG Kit layered approach for service abstractions.

6.1.2.1 Cloud versus Grid

The evolution of distributed systems has shifted from infrastructure-oriented architecture to service-oriented architecture. Figure 6.2 shows this change in perspective in detail. With the advent of networking technologies, the style of computing has also changed. The collaboration of services deployed across different computing networks and the capability of using these services without platform or infrastructure limitations have shifted computing to a large scale.

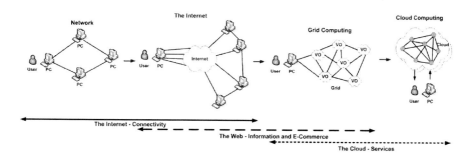

FIGURE 6.2: The evolution of the distributed computing paradigm from the perspective of the Internet infrastructure.

Apart from the systems point of view, cloud computing also has its origin from the Internet infrastructural perspective. The cloud computing capability is derived from the advancement of Internet and web technologies. In addition, cloud computing has benefited from the rapid development of communication technologies. Through large-scale network deployments, such as a grid, wide-area networks (WAN), and the Internet, users are able to do large-scale computations using either dedicated or shared network resources.

6.1.2.1.1 Definitions The term *grid computing* was coined in the mid-1990s to describe technologies that allow consumers to obtain computing resources on demand. These services were initially intended for advanced science and engineering applications. A well-structured definition of cloud computing was introduced by Foster et al. [76]: *"A large-scale distributed computing paradigm that is driven by economies of scale, in which a pool of abstracted, virtualized, dynamically scalable, managed computing power, storage, platforms, and services are delivered on demand to external customers over the Internet."*

Cloud computing can be differentiated from other existing distributed systems in the following ways:

- Cloud computing is massively scalable. Resources can be instantaneously added and/or removed.

- Cloud computing is driven by economies of scale.

- Cloud computing can deliver different levels of services to customers and offers abstraction of implementation, i.e., users are unaware of the details of the underlying application deployment.

6.1.2.1.2 Cloud addresses grid limitations Heterogeneity is an important issue in grid computing implementations. Large sets of heterogeneous hardware and software owned by different organizations with different usage policies pose a challenge to grid-based applications. Middleware applications and libraries on top of the grid fabric offer a mechanism for homogenization. However, difficulties still arise in cross-grid applications that run across different numbers of virtual organizations (VOs). In normal configurations, users are likely to be entangled in complex resource management and facilitation tasks.

In contrast, cloud systems emerged to provide a determined set of capabilities to the users; interface is the purpose of the design. These systems are often developed using a top-down design, in which the usability of the interface, i.e., the application, is the primary goal. Furthermore, cloud systems can be developed on top of existing grid infrastructures. Table 6.1 shows some of the differences between cloud and grid systems, as described by Foster et al. [76].

TABLE 6.1: Similarities and Differences between Cloud and Grid Systems

Perspective	Grid	Cloud
Design	Bottom up: From existing heterogeneous resources to development of abstraction layers for general usage.	Top-down: From interface design towards hardware and computing resources development and management.
Business Model	Project-oriented: Users have an allocation of service units that they can spend.	Consumption basis: Customers pay providers for the amount of services used.
Application Model	Support different types of applications: From high performance computing (HPC) to high throughput computing (HTC).	Support different types of applications: However, it is unlikely to support HPC applications. Applications can be loosely coupled, transaction-oriented, and interactive.
Compute Model	Batch-scheduled: Users submit batch jobs (via GRAM) to request resources for a period of time.	Interactive: Resources are shared by all users at the same time.
Data Model	Virtual data in data grids: Virtual data captures the relationship between data, programs, and computations and prescribes various abstractions within the data grid.	Data are shared between cloud and client computing

6.1.2.2 Cloud Services

Cloud services are usually provided at three different levels, namely infrastructure, platform, and software. Infrastructure as a Service (IaaS) offers hardware, software and other equipment to deliver application environments with a resource usage-based pricing model. An example of this type of service is Amazon's Elastic Cloud Computing (EC2). These services provide public access to computing and storage resources under pay-per-use model. In IaaS, the cloud infrastructure scales according to the application resource requirements.

Platform as a Service (PaaS) provides users the capability of developing and deploying custom applications on the cloud. PaaS provides an integrated environment for software development and testing. An example of PaaS is Google's App Engine, which enables users to build web-based applications for systems that run Google applications.

Software as a Service (SaaS) focuses on providing special-purpose software that consumers can access through the Internet based on a usage-based pricing model. An example of this type of service is Salesforce.com. Salesforce.com offers CRM (Customer Relationship Management) services. At present, Salesforce.com also delivers IaaS and PaaS services.

A wide range and variety of applications can be deployed on a cloud infrastructure. Consequently, data distribution and organization must be highly efficient. However, highly scalable data management schemes are in their infancy. Our aim is to offer a solution for existing data management schemes that are highly scalable and adaptive to dynamic changes in the applications environment of the cloud.

Cloud systems overcome the limitations of existing grid implementations by providing different levels of services in response to the users' requirements. Cloud systems can be deployed on top of existing grid infrastructures by providing an abstraction interface, which hides its complexities from the users. It is our hope that the future of cloud computing includes greater utilization of existing grid infrastructure.

6.1.3   Peer-to-Peer (P2P) Computing

The term *"peer-to-peer (P2P) computing"* was coined during the turn of the twenty-first century and refers to a system that utilizes distributed resources to perform functions in a fully decentralized manner. The P2P computing model enables direct resource sharing between peers [77]. This capability makes a system built on the P2P platform cost efficient and effective. In grid computing, the participants might be clusters or high performance desktops that are administered under a well-defined policy and trust. In contrast, a P2P community comprises diverse and anonymous participants with fewer restrictions. A node can join and leave a P2P network without facing any bureaucracy, and some P2P networks can scale up to hundreds of thousands or even millions of peers. More scalability means that more resources can be shared. Unfortunately, this scalability comes with the trade-off of a dynamic network. However, the peers in most of the available P2P systems are self-organized and are able to recover automatically in the event of peer failure. A P2P network operates without a server, i.e., all communicating peers are equal, which reduces the risk of a single point of failure. The fault tolerance of the system is ensured through data redundancy. A P2P network is more economical than a centralized or grid-based system because there is no server, which is expensive to acquire and maintain, and the peers are not required to be powerful machines with better connections, which must be maintained. However, P2P networks are challenged by data within the network because there is no authority to monitor the network. Specifically, several issues arise in file-sharing such as content pollution, out-of-control dissemination of sensitive data, malicious peers, and copyright infringement.

P2P computing provides an alternative to existing client-server models. It has a scalable resource sharing capability. Figure 6.3 compares a high-level view of interconnectivity in a P2P computing model with a client-server approach. Current research efforts in P2P computing are focused on the development of a dynamic file-sharing system. However, its real potential could lie

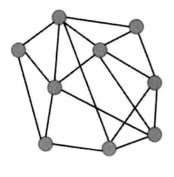 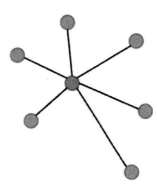

FIGURE 6.3: High-level views of a P2P computing model (left) and a client-server model (right).

far beyond this simple function. It might be possible to use P2P for complex operations, such as collaborative processing, in large-scale problems.

Some of the goals for the P2P system described in [78] include the following:

- *Cost sharing/reduction*: Reduces the operational costs associated with large and centralized resources by distributing these resources to peers.

- *Improved scalability/reliability*: The scalability and reliability of P2P systems are enhanced using innovative algorithms for resource discovery and search.

- *Resource aggregation and interoperability*: Because of its ability to aggregate resources, computationally expensive applications can be efficiently performed in a P2P system, e.g., distributed systems such as SETI@home.

- *Increased autonomy*: Each node in a P2P system has full autonomy on the resources that reside on the network, without depending on a central server.

- *Anonymity/privacy*: Users can hide their profiles.

- *Dynamism*: The computing environment within a P2P system is assumed to be highly dynamic, i.e., resources, such as compute nodes, continuously enter and leave the system.

- *Enabling ad-hoc communication and collaboration*: The dynamism of P2P systems allows for ad hoc communication and peer-to-peer collaboration.

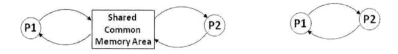

FIGURE 6.4: Inter-process communication approaches for a distributed computing environment.

6.2   Parallel Programming Techniques

In this section, we will briefly discuss two parallel programming domains that are commonly used in distributed computing environments: message passing interface (MPI) and graphical processing unit (GPU) programming. These programming techniques enable communications between processes to be performed in a distributed and parallel manner and allow these processes to use shared or distributed resources across the entire computational network.

6.2.1   Message-Passing Scheme

Message-passing is a communication procedure through which two or more processes share information. This approach is a type of inter-process communication, in which information is shared by means of message communications. Message-passing is different from the shared data approach, in that each process is capable of sending and receiving information rather than accessing a common repository of shared data (see Figure 6.4).

A message-passing system provides a set of message-based inter-process communication (IPC) protocols, which shield the details of complex network protocols and multiple heterogeneous platforms from programmers. The system enables processes to communicate by exchanging messages. Message-passing programs are written using simple communication primitives, such as *send* and *receive*. The message-passing scheme serves as a suitable infrastructure for building higher level IPC systems, such as RPC (Remote Procedure Call) and DSM (Distributed Shared Memory).

There are a number of desirable features for a good message-passing scheme. These include the following:

- *Simplicity*: The scheme should be easy to understand and comprehend. It should not have complex communication procedures. The sole purpose of message passing is to ensure information can be exchanged between one or more processes.

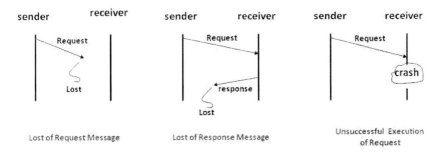

FIGURE 6.5: Different types of failures in message communication.

- *Uniform semantics*: Local and remote communications should implement similar primitives for data exchange.

- *Efficiency*: A good message-passing scheme minimizes the number of messages communicated between processes. For efficiency, some optimization is typically adopted. For example, avoiding the cost of establishing and terminating connections between the same pair of processes for each and every message exchange between them; minimizing the cost of maintaining connections; and piggybacking the acknowledgment of a previous message on the next message.

- *Reliability*: Message passing schemes must be able to handle lost and duplicate messages. Fault tolerance and error control approaches should be considered. There are three types of communication failures that require full consideration by the message passing system developers: lost request message, lost response message, and unsuccessful execution of the request. Figure 6.5 illustrates each of these failures.

6.2.1.1 Message Passing Interface (MPI)

Message Passing Interface (MPI) is a set of specifications that details the message passing libraries for developers and users. MPI by itself is not a library. It is the specification of what such a library should be. The goal of Message Passing Interface is to provide a widely used standard for writing message passing programs. The interface provides a practical, portable, efficient, and flexible standard for the development of message passing applications.

For the development of parallel programs, MPI offers a number of benefits: standardization, portability, performance opportunities, enhanced functionality, and different forms of availability. In the context of standardization, MPI is the only message passing library considered to be a standard. It is supported by all major platforms and many specialized high-performance computing (HPC) systems. Practically, it has replaced all previous message passing libraries, such as OpenMP. Developers are not required to modify message

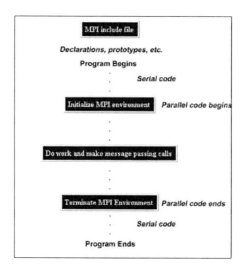

FIGURE 6.6: General MPI program structure

passing source code when porting a program to a platform that supports or is compliant with the MPI standard. In addition, MPI offers great functionality for message passing. In MPI version 1 (MPI-1), there are over 115 message passing routines. In MPI-2, these routines have been extended to include other key functionalities, such as dynamic processes, one-sided communication, and parallel I/O. There are a variety of MPI implementations available through both the vendor and public domains. These include *MPICH/MPICH-2* (Argonne National Laboratory), *LAM MPI* (Indiana University, USA), and *OpenMPI* (collaborative project between academic and business institutions).

MPI is native to the ANSI C programming language. However, there have been several initiatives to implement MPI using languages such as C++ (MPI-2 provides such capability, see [57]) and Java [79]. Figure 6.6 shows a common MPI program structure.

The MPI specification lends itself to virtually any distributed memory parallel programming model. In addition, MPI is commonly used to implement (behind the scenes) shared memory models, such as data parallelism, on distributed memory architectures. MPI can be executed on different hardware platforms, e.g., distributed memory, shared memory, or even hybrid shared-distributed systems. In the MPI implementation, all parallelism is explicit, i.e., the programmer is responsible for identifying parallelism and implementing parallel algorithms using MPI constructs. In addition, the number of tasks dedicated to run a parallel program is static. New tasks cannot be dynamically

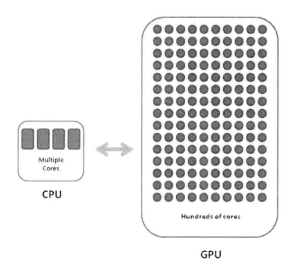

FIGURE 6.7: Comparison of the number of CPU and GPU cores (adapted from [80]).

spawned during run time. This limitation was addressed by MPI-2 specification.

6.2.2 GPU Programming

GPU programming is a set of tools and techniques for developing GPU computing applications. For scientific and engineering applications, GPU computing utilizes the graphical processing unit as a co-processor to accelerate CPU performances. This is achieved by off-loading computationally intensive and time-consuming portions of the programming code from CPU to GPU. From the user's perspective, applications run faster when the massively parallel processing power of GPU is harnessed.

Compared with the CPU, GPU contains more core processing units that are smaller in size. A typical CPU consists of four to eight cores, while a GPU comprises hundreds of smaller cores. Figure 6.7 shows an abstract comparison between CPU and GPU cores (adopted from [80]). As an example, the Intel Xeon processor has 108 million transistors, while the Radeon R300 GPU has 110 million transistors, and the GeForce FX GPU has 125 million transistors [81]. The numbers of transistors in these GPU units outnumber those in current CPUs.

In regards to the programming perspective, there are two parallel programming models that are commonly used to implement GPU applications. These are CUDA by NVIDIA and OpenCL.

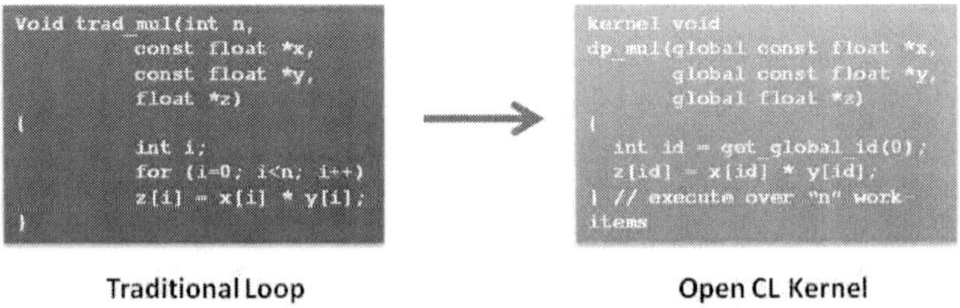

```
Void trad_mul(int n,                  kernel void
       const float *x,                dp_mul(global const float *x,
       const float *y,                       global const float *y,
       float *z)                             global float *z)
{                                     {
       int i;                                int id = get_global_id(0);
       for (i=0; i<n; i++)                   z[id] = x[id] * y[id];
       z[i] = x[i] * y[i];            } // execute over "n" work-
}                                     items
```

Traditional Loop   Open CL Kernel

FIGURE 6.8: Conversion of a normal loop condition to an OpenCL kernel.

6.2.2.1   CUDA

CUDA is a set of proprietary API and language extensions for GPU programming that works on NVIDIA's GPUs. CUDA can be used via the runtime API or the hardware API [82]. The runtime API provides C-like routines and extensions for application development. The hardware API provides more flexibility, in that it offers low-level control of hardware, but requires more code and programming effort. Both CUDA and OpenCL implement a piece of code that runs on GPU, known as the kernel. CUDA can be written in high-level programming languages such as C, C++, and Fortran.

6.2.2.2   OpenCL

Open Computing Language (OpenCL) [83] is a GPU programming model that can be used on multiple platforms. OpenCL implements a C-like language for programming compute device programs. The key feature of OpenCL is portability. Unlike a CUDA kernel, an OpenCL kernel can be compiled at runtime, which would add to an OpenCL's running time. Because OpenCL is intended for different GPU platforms, its kernel can be developed based on the specific platform to be used. Figure 6.8 shows the conversion of a sequential program to OpenCL.

6.3   From Coding to Applications

In this chapter, we have discussed system models and programming languages that can be used to develop Internet-scale applications. By harnessing the tremendous potentials of the distributed system architecture, which range from high-speed Internet connectivity to inter-process communications in GPU computing, we are able to develop scalable systems that can adapt to the scale of data. Because we are moving rapidly toward extremely large scale data generation, scalability is an important issue to be addressed. It has been reported that Amazon Web Services (AWS) estimates that its S3 storage service will soon have more than a trillion objects in storage and be capable of handling a million requests per second [84]. Therefore, distributed and parallel programming techniques and models must be developed for future system and application developers.

Part IV

Implementations and Applications

Chapter 7

Multi-Feature Classifications for Complex Data

Pattern recognition involves a set of processes to define similarities and/or differences between two or more patterns. Patterns or data must be evaluated or measured to find distinctive characteristics. The first step in any pattern recognition scheme is to identify measurable quantities or characteristics of patterns that match a specific class of data. These measurable quantities are known as features. According to Theodoridis and Koutroumbas [85], features can be defined as a set of measurements used for recognition and classification. These measurements form a feature vector that is used for recognition purposes. In image recognition, examples of features include colors, edges, and spectrum frequencies.

Pattern recognition, as described in the previous chapters, is a series of processes including data acquisition, data pre-processing, and classification [86]. Each data presented for recognition is assigned to the data class that most closely matches the features of the data. These features are extracted before any classification/recognition process takes place. The extraction process is performed during the pre-processing stage of pattern recognition. In existing pattern recognition schemes, the number of features used tends to be very large. A phenomenon known as the *"curse of dimensionality"* arises as a result of the high dimensionality of the computational space.

This chapter focuses on pattern recognition schemes involving multiple features. A multiple-feature implementation enables a holistic approach to the pattern recognition procedure that takes into consideration all significant features representing a particular set of patterns, such as images and sensor readings. This multi-feature consideration is important when considering complex data in an Internet-scale environment. The multi-feature approach was designed to reduce the bias effect caused by selecting only a single feature for classification/recognition purposes. To avoid the curse of dimensionality, current approaches in pattern recognition require a significant amount of effort to analyze different forms of features. This effort limits their ability to seamlessly and effectively perform recognition and classification on complex data sets. Furthermore, the computational complexity of most existing schemes inhibits their ability to scale up to an increasing number of features.

It is envisioned that the distributed approach can be implemented in Internet-scale pattern recognition involving multiple features. It is argued that a set of distributed computational networks working collaboratively can scale the pattern recognition scheme in response to an increasing number of features. In addition, the performance of this multi-feature scheme can be improved by a single-cycle learning distributed pattern recognition algorithm, such as the DHGN. In contrast to other contemporary machine learning approaches, our approach allows induction of new patterns in a fixed number of steps. While doing so, it exhibits a high level of scalability, i.e., the performance and accuracy do not degrade as the number of stored patterns increases. The pattern recognition capability remains comparable with contemporary approaches, such as the support vector machine (SVM), self-organizing map (SOM), and artificial neural network (ANN). Furthermore, all computations are completed within the pre-defined number of steps. The one-shot learning in this method is achieved by sidestepping the commonly used error/energy minimization and random walk approaches. The network functions as a matrix that holds all possible solutions for the problem domain. The DHGN approach finds and refines the initial solution by passing the results through a pyramidal hierarchy of similar arrays. In doing so, it eliminates/resolves pattern defects; distortions up to 20% are tolerated [64]. Previously encountered patterns are revealed and new patterns are memorized without the loss of stored information. In fact, the pattern recognition accuracy continues to improve as the network processes more sensory inputs [3].To achieve this goal, the DHGN distributed pattern recognition algorithm is extended for multi-feature recognition and the analysis of complex data.

7.1   Data Features for Pattern Recognition

Consider the data representation shown in Figure 7.1. Using the mean pixel value as a feature for a set of images, we are considering the following one-dimensional problem: determine to which class a particular image belongs. However, as another feature is added, e.g., the standard deviation of the pixel value, additional computation is required to determine the correlations between features that produce distinctive classes of images. As more features are added, the computational costs of determining the correlations become progressively higher. According to Theodoridis and Koutroumbas [85], although two features may carry good classification if treated separately, their high mutual correlations implies that there is little gained by combining these features in the feature vector. The increased complexity does not benefit the recognition process.

In classification algorithms of existing pattern recognition schemes, the number of features directly translates to the number of classifier parameters. Therefore, increasing the number of features leads to complexity. The

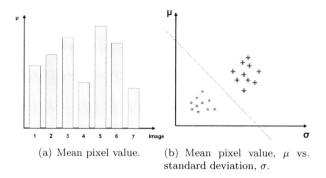

(a) Mean pixel value.   (b) Mean pixel value, μ vs. standard deviation, σ.

FIGURE 7.1: Data feature representation for a set of images.

algorithm must determine and continue to adjust synaptic weights during the recognition process [87]. To ensure the efficiency of the recognition scheme, it is imperative that the number of features be kept to a minimum. Nevertheless, selecting features for recognition is a complex process that needs to be performed objectively.

To address the curse of dimensionality, current approaches extend the recognition process by introducing a feature selection mechanism to select the features that best represent the entire data set. However, dimensionality reduction adds to the complexity of the recognition processes and requires the use of costly algorithms, such as the principal component analysis (PCA). Furthermore, erroneous feature selection can affect the accuracy of the recognition scheme. A simple recognition scheme that is capable of analyzing more than one feature and does not use a feature selection mechanism to determine the best features for data representation is needed.

7.2   Distributed Multi-Feature Recognition

The scalability of commonly used pattern recognition techniques involving multiple features usually deteriorates as the number of training and testing data sets increases. In this chapter, we will look at multi-feature recognition by including the distributiveness that occurs in natural schemes. The DHGN algorithm has been modeled with a fully distributed approach for recognition using multiple data features. The following subsections will describe the distributed DHGN scheme for multi-feature recognition.

The DHGN multi-feature scheme conducts distributed pattern recognition using features obtained from pattern data through a feature extraction method. It provides a scalable approach; the number of features required for

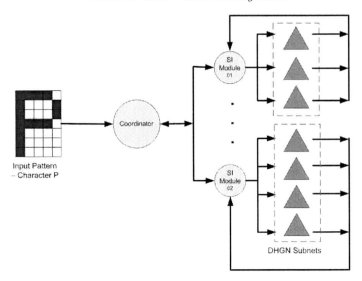

FIGURE 7.2: DHGN multi-feature recognition scheme, a collection of DHGN networks that analyze patterns using multiple sets of features.

recognition can be extended provided sufficient computational resources are available. The number of features, f, is directly proportional to the computational resources available for the recognition scheme, c; $f \propto c$. These resources are in the form of distributed computational networks, which provide greater scalability for recognition purposes.

7.2.1 Conceptual Design and Implementation

The design for multi-feature recognition comprises a collection of DHGN networks. Each network performs a distributed recognition scheme for a single feature. Figure 7.2 presents the DHGN multi-feature recognition approach.

In this configuration, a coordinator node is used for data acquisition and networks coordination. This node communicates the patterns received to the SI module node on each DHGN network. Each SI module has a copy of the pattern set for the recognition process. The SI module starts the recognition process by generating a single feature obtained from the input patterns. The feature data are used as a pattern for recognition purposes. The rest of the recognition procedures in each network are similar to the original DHGN scheme. The results for each recognition process conducted by each DHGN network are sent to its respective SI module. Each SI module produces a result for the recognition/classification of each pattern in context with the operator-specific accuracy parameter(s). These parameters can include recall, precision, and error values. The results are passed to coordinator node, and the error is calculated. The error per test object, P_{err}, for a given number of test objects o_t is calculated for each feature using the following equation:

$$P_{err} = \frac{F_{+ve} + F_{-ve}}{o_t} \qquad (7.1)$$

where F_{+ve} and F_{-ve} represent the number of false positives and negatives, respectively.

The following scenario illustrates recognition accuracy calculations based on error values. There are a series of patterns, P, containing n classes, $P = \{p_1, p_2, \ldots, p_n\}$, and a set of features, $F = \{f_1, f_2, \ldots, f_m\}$. For each pattern class, p_x, $x = 1, 2, \ldots, n$, select the feature, f_y, $y = 1, 2, \ldots, m$ that minimizes the recognition error, err_{f_x}, for all test patterns. The recall accuracy, r_{p_x}, for each pattern class is derived using the following equation:

$$r_{p_x} = \arg\min\left\{err_{f_1} : err_{f_m}\right\}, \quad x = 1, 2, \ldots, n \qquad (7.2)$$

Note that the minimum error is not the only parameter that can be used to determine the most effective recall accuracy for multi-feature pattern recognition. Other parameters include the normal mean, median, standard deviation, and other statistical estimations, such as Bayes and maximum-likelihood estimators.

7.2.2 Complexity Estimation

In multi-feature recognition using the DHGN distributed pattern recognition (DPR) scheme, the approach applied to recognizing features in each pattern is similar to the original DHGN implementation described in Chapter 5. Therefore, the complexity of the basic recognition function (for recognition at the subpattern level) is as low as the originally proposed scheme. However, in the multi-feature scheme, the voting mechanism is applied at two levels, i.e., at the SI module and the coordinator nodes.

At the SI module node, voting determines the matched pattern class for a given pattern. At the coordinator node, voting selects the feature that gives the optimal value for the specified accuracy parameter.

7.2.2.1 Voting Scheme at the SI Module

The voting scheme applied at the SI module assigns the test pattern into a specific pattern class, based on a similar characteristic or feature value. Inputs to this voting process are the indices retrieved from all of the DHGN subnets. Each SI module handles a specific feature for a particular dataset. The maximum voting scheme in this DHGN implementation finds the maximum number of similar indices returned from the subnets. The voting scheme has two stages, namely vote counting and maximum vote search.

In the vote counting process, the SI module performs an index-matching process to compare the index obtained from the test pattern with the indices of patterns stored for each pattern class. The following pseudocode illustrates this process:

Algorithm 3 SI Module Voting Scheme

1: **for** $i = 1$ to MaxTestPatternNo **do**
2:    **for** $j = 1$ to MaxSubnetNo **do**
3:       **for** $k = 1$ to MaxStoredPatternNo **do**
4:          **if** $i.index \equiv k.index$ **then**
5:             $k.vote + +$
6:          **end if**
7:       **end for**
8:    **end for**
9: **end for**

The complexity of this process can be further analyzed using a Big-O analysis. We can deduce that the complexity of the vote-counting process is n-polynomial, where $n = 3$. Given a vote-counting function $f(v_{cnt})$, its complexity in Big-O notation is as follows:

$$f(v_{cnt}) = O(n^3) \tag{7.3}$$

Where n represents a single executable instruction in the function. After the numbers of votes are counted, the SI module performs a search function to identify the pattern class that has the highest votes for the tested pattern. This function will execute a linear search to find the maximum number of votes.

7.2.2.2   Voting Scheme at the Coordinator Node

The voting scheme at the coordinator node is used to select the best accuracy parameter of a feature from a collection of available features that have been used in earlier recognition schemes implemented on multiple DHGN networks. Each SI module will communicate the results of the recognition of features as patterns to the coordinator node for further analysis. The coordinator stores all of the accuracy parameters received from the SI modules. Table 7.1 shows a sample of errors obtained from two SI module nodes for each feature, on five different pattern classes.

Based on the values obtained from Table 7.1, we can conclude that Feature 1 is the best feature to represent pattern classes 1, 3, and 4 because its errors are less than the errors of Feature 2. Pattern classes 2 and 5 are likely to be represented by Feature 2. The voting function in the coordinator node

TABLE 7.1: Examples of Data Obtained from SI Modules, in the Form of Errors for Each Feature

Feature	Pattern Class				
	1	2	3	4	5
1	5.26	4.25	1.78	0.85	3.99
2	21.03	3.25	9.36	10.05	2.01

represents linear search complexity. The following pseudocode outlines the coordinator's voting function:

Algorithm 4 Coordinator Voting Scheme

1: $MinFeature = 99.99$
2: **for** $i = 1$ to MaxPatternClass **do**
3:    **for** $j = 1$ to MaxFeatureNo **do**
4:       **if** $i.j.FeatErr \leq MinFeature$ **then**
5:          $MinFeature = i.j.FeatErr$
6:       **end if**
7:    **end for**
8: **end for**

This algorithm is used to find the minimum error obtained from the recognition process for each feature. Similar to the vote counting function in the SI module nodes, we can derive a Big-O notation for the coordinator's voting function, $f(v_{min})$ as a n-polynomial function with executable instructions, $n = 2$. Therefore, the following Big-O notation applies:

$$f(v_{min}) = O(n^2) \tag{7.4}$$

Figure 7.3 shows the estimated execution time for the voting function for 10,000 pattern classes as a function of the number of features used, n_{feat}. It is assumed that the computation time of an instruction is 1 µs. Note that the minimum voting function takes only one second to select the lowest error from 100 features on 10,000 pattern classes (trained patterns). This voting process exhibits higher scalability for recognition through the distribution of recognition procedure on a group of collaborative DHGN networks.

The DHGN multi-feature recognition scheme allows recognition to be performed in a scalable manner, extending its capability of using multiple pattern features in the recognition procedure. By having a distributed architecture in the recognition scheme, the DHGN provides an avenue for recognition/classification to be executed in a highly scalable manner, while maintaining its low computational complexity. However, the proposed pre- and

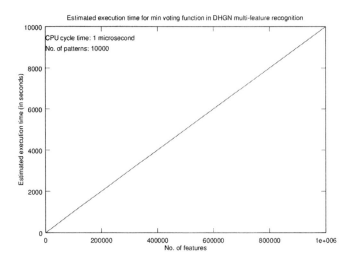

FIGURE 7.3: Estimated execution time for minimum voting function in the coordinator node for 10,000 pattern classes as a function of the number of features.

post-processing mechanisms described in this section do not entail a rigid framework. Different types of data analysis and feature extraction can be accommodated in this scheme. The DHGN multi-feature scheme is considered to be commodity application that can be used in different application domains.

7.3 Handwritten Object Classification with Multiple Features

In this section, we demonstrate the capabilities of the DHGN distributed scheme as a single classifier for combined multi-feature pattern recognition on handwritten character objects. A comparative evaluation with previous work performed by Duin and Tax [88] will be discussed. Note that this work on the DHGN multi-feature scheme is not intended to showcase an optimal solution with high accuracy for complex pattern recognition. Rather, this study was carried out to provide an alternative scalable pattern recognition scheme for multi-feature patterns.

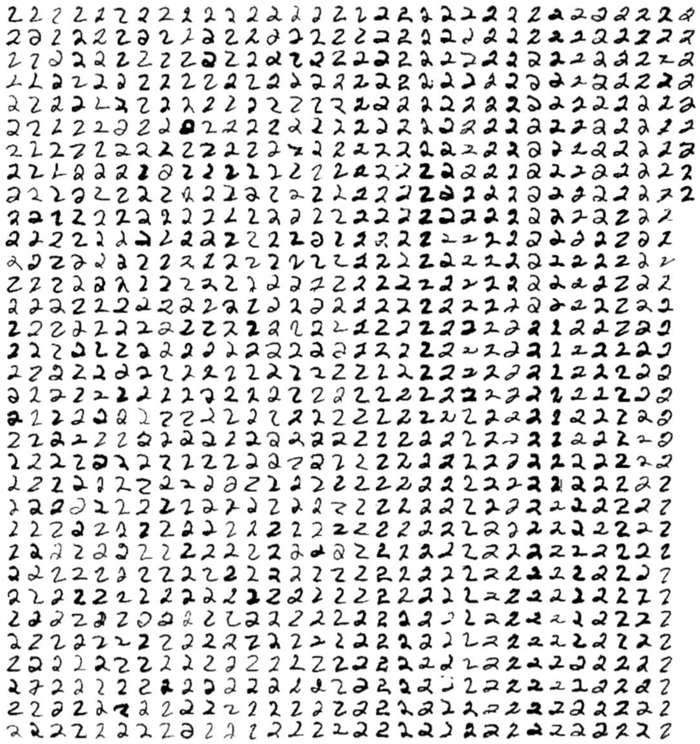

FIGURE 7.4: MNIST character "2" data set.

7.3.1 Handwritten Object

A handwritten object is a character representation based on a set of lines and strokes captured by an optical reader during a manual handwriting process. Some of the basic features of handwritten objects include aspect ratio, pixel percentages, number of strokes and position of the character on the specified axes. To classify handwritten objects, a recognition procedure is conducted using one or more of these features. Because of patterns complexity, the recognition process for handwritten objects takes into account more than one feature. Some of the available handwritten object data sets also use other numerical features, such as Fourier coefficients, Zernike moments, and morphological features.

There are a number of handwritten object databases available, including the MNIST database introduced by LeCun et al. [89]. Figure 7.4 shows a training data set for the character "2" of the MNIST data set.

One of the commonly used data sets is the handwritten numeral characters extracted from a set of Dutch utility maps. This data set comprises ten classes

TABLE 7.2: Discretization of Feature Data Using Variable-Binning Methods

Feature	min	max	μ	Bins				
				1	2	3	4	5
Zernike	0.0011	777.86	88.64	$\leq$25	26-50	51-90	91-400	401-800
Fourier	0.0002	0.7965	0.1320	$\leq$ 0.001	0.002-0.05	0.06-0.14	0.15-0.50	0.51-0.80

of characters ranging from numerals "0" to "9." Each class holds 200 objects. It is publicly available from the UCI Machine Learning Repository [90].

7.3.2   Classification Procedures

The classification process in our proposed DHGN multi-feature scheme involves a series of single-cycle stages that have been applied to the feature data set of numeral characters described earlier. A three-stage process was considered in the recognition scheme: feature pre-processing, recognition, and results evaluation. It should be noted that our proposed scheme implements a single-classifier for multi-feature recognition. The following subsection will detail out these implementation stages.

7.3.2.1   Stage 1: Feature Pre-Processing

In the pre-processing stage, all selected features undergo a discretization process to transform continuous feature values into a discrete format. This process is a pre-requisite for the existing DHGN scheme that implements the recognition procedure using discrete-format data.

Discretization was performed on the feature set using a binning approach. For each feature set, a number of bins (thresholds) were defined within a range of values. These bins were created based on the parameter values obtained from the whole feature set. Table 7.2 shows a sample of the bins defined for two of handwritten object features: Zernike moments and Fourier coefficients.

The discretization process reduces the feature data composition by transforming the feature set from a continuous to a discrete data space. This reduces the complexity of the data set used in the recognition procedure. However, because the actual values are lost during the conversion, the discretization process results in an inaccurate data representation.

The output of the discretization process is a set of patterns for each feature. These patterns correspond to the test objects used in the tests. Table 7.3 shows a sample of patterns for the Zernike moment feature obtained from the discretization process. The size of the patterns reflects the number of values/coefficients for each feature; the dimension of patterns corresponds to the number of bins, i.e., 5.

TABLE 7.3: Pattern Samples of the Zernike Moment Feature Obtained Using Discretization

Object ID	Feature Pattern
1	12343000132001234000030000400120033010033011400
2	01243000222001134001320022300220131012033011400
3	01243000121001234001200022400100130011034011400
4	12243000112001233001120023300120131001034002400
5	01143000122001234000120022300120132001033012400

7.3.2.2   Stage 2: Multi-Feature Recognition

In multi-feature recognition for multiple features of numeral character objects, each DHGN network performs recognition on a specific feature set. The sizes of the networks are not uniform.

The recognition process begins when the coordinator node communicates the feature patterns to the SI module node on each network according to the specific feature assigned to the DHGN network. The communications of patterns in this scheme follow the message-passing model described in Section 2.6.2.

The SI module node in each network divides and distributes the received patterns to the available subnets in the network. Each DHGN subnet initiates a recognition process at subpattern level. The results of each recognition process are sent back to the SI module node where the maximum voting process is used identify the best match pattern class for each pattern. After completing the voting process, the SI module determines the accuracy parameters used in the scheme. These parameters can include commonly used recognition accuracy parameters, such as precision rate, recall rate, accuracy level, and error value. These values are communicated to the coordinator node for the results evaluation stage.

7.3.2.3   Stage 3: Results Evaluation

The results evaluation stage determines the best or optimal feature to be selected as the best representative for each pattern class in the recognition scheme. This process occurs within the coordinator node. The values obtained from the SI module nodes are compared to the accuracy parameter(s). This evaluation stage of the DHGN multi-feature recognition applies a generic approach, and different sets of recognition accuracy parameters can be used in the classification process. This approach allows for flexibility in the decisions on classification, in that different accuracy factors can be observed and analyzed.

7.4   Distributed Multi-Feature Recognition Perspective

Given the extensive capabilities of existing data capture technologies to retrieve and generate complex data, it is important to consider a multi-feature approach for pattern recognition. Existing scheme are not able to scale up with the enormous Internet-scale data. A distributed perspective in implementing pattern recognition is required. In this chapter, we have discussed a number of benefits in implementing a distributed pattern recognition scheme, including the following:

1. A distributed approach for pattern recognition, such as the DHGN, allows more features to be used in the recognition process, e.g., by allocating an additional DHGN network for each feature recognition.

2. The single classifier mechanism of the DHGN can be used for any number of features. In contrast, existing multi-feature schemes merely implement combined-classifiers for classification.

In this chapter, we have presented a distributed approach for multi-feature pattern recognition. The implementation of a single-cycle learning DHGN algorithm for distributed feature analysis on a collaborative computational network was discussed. The proposed approach implements a single classifier scheme for different feature sets. This is achieved using a divide-and-distribute approach on the available features for each data set. The proposed approach is not affected by the curse of dimensionality, which results from multiple features. By allowing features to be added to the analysis using available computational networks, the DHGN approach implements a scalable recognition scheme.

Chapter 8

Pattern Recognition within Coarse-Grained Networks

A distinctive difference between conventional and distributed pattern recognition is the resource consideration. In a distributed approach, the system must be capable of utilizing the available resources effectively and efficiently. A good communication model must be considered to ensure proper utilization and communication of resources between processing nodes. Distributed pattern recognition (DPR) has the ability to scale up the process as the size of the problem increases. However, the scalability depends on the resource availability in a particular computational network. Resource availability is influenced by the capacity and stability of the computational network. The network capacity in distributed applications, such as DPR, is observed in terms of the granularity of the network. Commonly, computational networks are either coarse-grained, such as a computational grid, or fine-grained, such as a wireless sensor network (WSN). The processing capacities and capabilities of these networks differ. Because the application deployment focused on a single problem domain, most existing pattern recognition schemes are non-adaptive to different network granularities. The DHGN pattern recognition scheme described in Chapter 5 was developed with adaptive network granularity consideration [4] and the algorithm can be deployed in both coarse- and fine-grained networks.

In this chapter, we will look at the network granularity aspect of distributed pattern recognition (DPR). We will demonstrate how the DHGN algorithm can be deployed in a network of different granularity, which allows for flexible recognition of different forms of Internet-scale data. In addition, we will discuss specific pattern recognition applications in coarse-grained networks.

8.1 Network Granularity Considerations

Granularity of a computational network refers to the levels of its composition. A coarse-grained network mainly consists of a few large processing entities, which are capable of handling significantly high computational loads. An example of this type of network is a computational grid network. Con-

TABLE 8.1: Comparison of Fine- and Coarse-Grained Network Specifications

	Network Granularity	
Specifications	Coarse-Grained	Fine-Grained
No. of Processing Nodes	Low to High	High
Processing Capacity	High	Low
Storage Capacity	High	Low
Energy Supply	High	Low
Example	Computational Grid	WSN

versely, fine-grained networks are defined as a network that comprises many small processing nodes that perform simple and lightweight tasks, such as the wireless sensor network (WSN). Table 8.1 compares the specifications of coarse- and fine-grained computational networks.

The DHGN implementation for distributed pattern recognition takes into account these two levels of granularity. This is essential in providing a scalable and robust scheme that can be used in different network conditions. Furthermore, because of the network granularity considerations, the DHGN algorithm is made aware of the resource availability of the computational network to be used in the recognition process.

8.1.1   DHGN Configurations for Adaptive Granularity

Two configurations for the DHGN implementation will be presented: fully distributed and clustered.

8.1.1.1   Fully Distributed Configuration

The original configuration of the DHGN algorithm described in Chapter 5 distributed all of the neurons in a DHGN subnet to the processing nodes. This implies that each node is responsible for a single neuron in a DHGN subnet. This configuration eliminates the requirement for high processing capability and storage capacity because the computing node performs the recognition process on a single atomic element of the input subpattern. However, the communication costs for each node require considerable attention. Each node is required to communicate frequently with other neighboring nodes to update its bias array. Figure 8.1 shows the fully distributed configuration of the DHGN algorithm for a WSN. Note that each neuron is mapped to a processing node. Processing nodes that are close together are grouped into individual DHGN subnets.

This fully distributed DHGN configuration can be deployed in a fine-grained network that comprises sensor nodes with restricted computing resources, such as WSN. A major challenge in this implementation is the rapid inter-node communications required for message exchange during the recognition process.

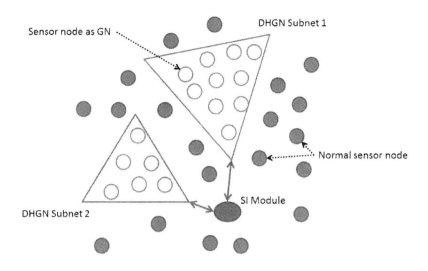

FIGURE 8.1: Fully distributed DHGN configuration for a fine-grained network.

The DHGN deployment must be able to perform single-hop communication between adjacent nodes for the message exchange process. To ensure that efficient energy-communication utilization is achieved during the recognition process, the physical distance should be taken into account when implementing the DHGN distributed recognition application in WSN. A DHGN deployment in fine-grained networks will be presented in the next chapter.

8.1.1.2 Clustered Configuration

The clustered configuration maps each DHGN subnet over a single processing node. Each node is capable of conducting the recognition process based on the input subpatterns obtained from the SI module node. In this configuration, the recognition process involves the entire input subpattern and the processing node is expected to acquire high processing capability and storage capacity. However, because the communication involves only message communication from the SI module node to each of the processing nodes, the communication costs between sensor nodes are minimized. Figure 8.2 shows the clustered configuration of the DHGN algorithm for WSN.

Each processing node in the clustered DHGN configuration can perform recognition on each subpattern independently. The node must be able to provide sufficient processing and storage capacity to conduct the recognition process. This configuration is intended to be used on coarse-grained networks,

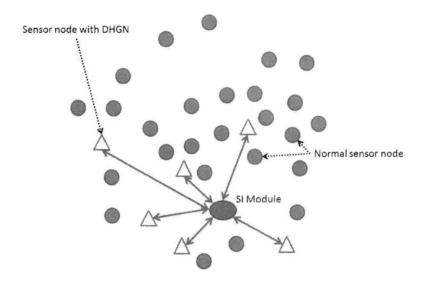

FIGURE 8.2: Clustered DHGN configuration for a coarse-grained network. Each DHGN node is capable of performing the entire subpattern recognition processes.

such as grid and cloud computing, in which additional processing and storage capacity can be made available.

An important benefit of having this DHGN cluster performed on a single processing node is that it eliminates all of the communication actions in the DHGN message-passing model for distributed systems. For each subpattern recognition process, each node communicates the index generated to the SI module. The absence of communication between nodes reduces the chances of recognition failures attributed to transmission or communication errors. When the clustered configuration is used to implement the DHGN, the DHGN subnets are formed using the internal memory structure of a single node. An associative array structure for each DHGN subnet was adopted. Table 8.2 shows the associative array structure for a DHGN subnet with 5-bit binary subpatterns.

Communications between each GN memory structure in the DHGN subnet are conducted using conventional value store/retrieve processes, which update values using value assignment.

8.1.2 DHGN Commodity Grid Framework

Distributed pattern recognition provides an avenue for achieving Internet-scale pattern recognition using a state-of-the-art data classifier for fast track-

TABLE 8.2: DHGN Subnet Associative Array Structure after Subpatterns 00001 and 11111 Have Been Memorized

GN ID	Row	Layer	Value	Bias Array	
				Index	Entry
1	1	0	0	1	#,1
2	1	0	0	1	1,1
3	1	0	0	1	1,1
4	1	0	0	1	1,2
5	1	0	0	-	-
6	2	0	1	1	#,2
7	2	0	1	1	2,2
8	2	0	1	1	2,2
9	2	0	1	1	2,2
10	2	0	1	1	1,#
				2	2,#
11	1	1	#	1	#,1,1
12	1	1	#	1	1,1,1
13	1	1	#	1	1,1,#
14	2	1	#	1	#,1,1
15	2	1	#	1	1,1,1
16	2	1	#	1	1,1,#
17	1	2	#	1	1
18	2	2	#	1	2

ing large-scale data analyses. A framework proposed by Muhamad Amin and Khan [55] employs a grid-enabled DHGN distributed pattern recognition scheme. The framework comprises a commodity-grid (CoG) network [74] for pattern recognition implementation using the DHGN approach. The commodity-grid provides an easy-to-use front-end for accessing a distributed system supporting complex operations.

The proposed framework for our distributed pattern recognition is a combination of a commodity-grid based architecture and the single-cycle learning DHGN associative memory approach for pattern recognition. The commodity grid infrastructure enables us to offer the pattern recognition service to multiple users from different expertise domains and application areas. For instance, climatic change research can use the proposed system for long-term climate pattern discovery, while the bioinformatics field can use this resource for protein structure recognition and classification. This extends the scalability of the DHGN DPR scheme across different application domains.

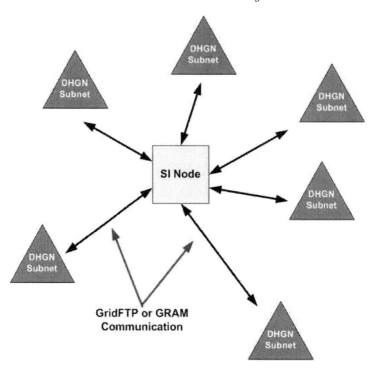

FIGURE 8.3: Proposed commodity grid-based distributed pattern recognition framework.

8.1.2.1 DPR Architecture

The system architecture for the pattern recognition application directly follows the DHGN clustered configuration described earlier. Figure 8.3 shows the grid network layout for the proposed framework.

Communication between the DHGN subnets and the SI module is performed using existing file transfer or resource allocation services, such as GridFTP or GRAM. Each DHGN subnet can be hosted by a single computing node, or group of nodes within a subnet. The communications between the nodes in each subnet are handled by a Message Passing Interface (MPI), which facilitates the parallel DHGN computations.

The proposed distributed pattern recognition is a real-time application that is able to produce the results in a single cycle of computations. Furthermore, each of the DHGN subnets executes independently, and thus provides a high level of scalability and efficiency by removing the requirement for inter-subnet communications. The SI role and a DHGN subnet role can be easily interchanged, i.e., any node in the grid can take over the SI role for the framework.

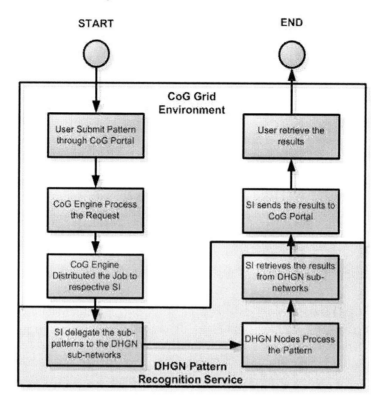

FIGURE 8.4: DPR-commodity grid workflow.

8.1.2.2 DPR Workflow

Workflow support is the key to diversifying this application as a generic resource for E-Research. Figure 8.4 illustrates the workflow for the proposed distributed pattern recognition framework.

The proposed framework utilizes both the commodity-grid processes and the core pattern recognition service. Note that the front-end of the system is managed by the CoG portal.

8.1.2.3 DPR-CoG Framework

Figure 8.5 shows the framework for implementing the distributed pattern recognition system. The framework is designed to cater to different types of users/applications that require flexible access to a large-scale low-latency pattern recognition resource. The CoG portal and engine provide the authentication and security services for the users.

The framework used in this study implements the Karajan CoG grid engine [91]. Figure 8.6 shows the Karajan architecture for a commodity grid.

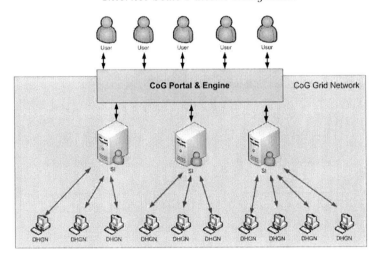

FIGURE 8.5: Framework for commodity-grid based pattern recognition.

The Karajan architecture offers additional libraries for the front-end design through its HTML and forms libraries. It uses the task library for grid integration, which is based on the Java CoG Kit abstractions.

8.2   Face Recognition Using the Multi-Feature DPR Approach

With the advent of Internet connectivity, the outgrowth of images produced and posted on the Web is tremendous in numbers. The nature of the images is diverse. Some images are taken by normal or highly specialized cameras and some, such as MRI and seismic images, are sophisticated and multi-dimensional. Images are used in a variety of fields, including arts, engineering, and sciences. Images are commonly used to recognize or detect objects, such as a human face.

Face recognition is a well-known application that implements pattern recognition concepts and approaches. Numerous computational designs and implementations have been proposed in the literature. Each of these approaches contributes to accuracy and/or efficiency of the application. In this section, we will present a distributed approach for face recognition using the multi-feature DHGN algorithm. Our intent is not to outweigh the capabilities of current and more establish facial recognition schemes, but to give an insight into how this complex operation on Internet-scale data can be performed in a distributed manner. Further details on the analysis of the recognition accu-

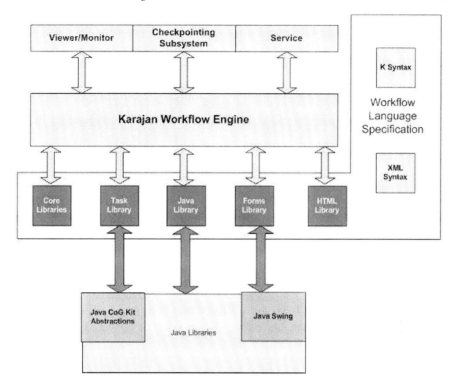

FIGURE 8.6: The Karajan grid engine architecture.

racy of the DHGN multi-feature scheme applied to face recognition have been presented in [92].

8.2.1 Color and Spatio-Structural Features Consideration

The DHGN multi-feature scheme takes a holistic approach to incorporating simultaneously the color and spatio-structural features into the recognition process. A binary signature scheme proposed by Nascimento and Chitkara [93] was adopted for content-based image retrieval (CBIR) in the pattern recognition procedure. This scheme integrates the global binary signature with an edge detection technique, such as Sobel's [94], for DHGN single-cycle image recognition. In this multi-feature recognition approach, any number of features can be included for pattern analysis by incorporating a sufficient number of DHGN networks.

8.2.1.1 Global Binary Signature Scheme for Color Recognition

A common approach used to represent color distributions of an image is the Global Color Histogram (GCH). Given an n-color model, a GCH is developed

Original Image   Edge Map

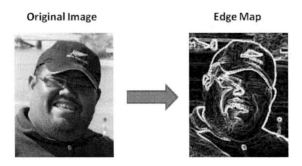

FIGURE 8.7: Edge map generated by applying Sobel's edge detection technique to an original gray-scale facial image.

with an n-dimensional feature vector, $\{p_1, p_2, \ldots, p_n\}$, where p_i represents the normalized percentage of color pixels that corresponds to each color element in an image. Nascimento and Chitkara [93] proposed an alternative approach for color distribution representation using a global binary signature scheme. It is a compact form of the existing GCH that uses binary bit-strings as a signature. This signature is an abstract representation of the image's color distribution. The bit-strings are of a pre-determined size, which makes it ideal for use in DHGN binary pattern representations.

8.2.1.2   Edge Detection for Structural Information

Edges provide important spatio-structural information for image recognition. This multi-feature DPR scheme includes edge detection in the color-based recognition process. The outputs from the edge detection process are represented as an edge map. Figure 8.7 shows the transformation of a gray-scale image to the corresponding edge map using Sobel's edge detection technique.

With the ability to capture and convert the two main features of an image, i.e., colors and edges, into binary patterns, the distributed multi-feature recognition scheme is able to apply a highly scalable single-cycle learning technique for binary patterns in a computational network for multi-feature pattern recognition. Any number of features can be included in the scheme provided a separate network is available for each feature (see Figure 7.2).

An interesting characteristic of the DHGN implementation for multi-feature recognition is the constant recall time for each feature. This characteristic is independent of the number of input patterns presented. Furthermore, the scheme minimizes the recall time. Figure 8.8 shows the overall store/recall times for each DHGN subnet in a face recognition simulation using 1000 images. In a simulated computation network, each DHGN subnet processed all

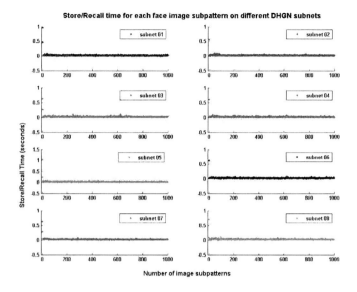

FIGURE 8.8: Store/recall times for each subpattern in each DHGN subnet during the edge recognition process.(With kind permission from Springer Science+Business Media: Neural Process. Lett., "Distributed Multi-Feature Recognition Scheme for Greyscale Images," vol. 33, issue 1, pp. 45-59, (February 2011), Muhamad Amin, A.H., and Khan, A.I., Fig.12, http://dx.doi.org/10.1007/s11063-010-9163-8.)

of the images in less than 30 seconds. The processing times will substantially be less for a real computational network with parallel processing resources. These speeds make it possible to process live image data streams and large data sets in real time.

The DHGN multi-feature scheme provides a highly efficient and scalable mechanism for multi-feature pattern recognition on coarse-grained computational networks. This multi-feature recognition approach represents a holistic process where more features can be taken into consideration without any changes to the approach. The scheme has shown to be highly scalable and the processing time and recognition accuracy are not adversely affected with the increase in number of processed patterns. The approach discussed in this section works well on gray-scale images and it can be applied to a number of fields that require gray-scale image analysis. The flexibility to include any image feature at any point creates a *"plug-and-play"* capability for dynamic image analysis. This scheme opens up the possibility for real-time image recognition on Internet-scale data sets in biomedical imaging and video streaming. Furthermore, through distribution of features, the DHGN is capable of performing the recognition process on patterns with increasing size and dimension. Note that the use of facial images in the recognition simulation does not imply that DHGN is a face recognition application with a promising high level of accuracy. Rather, the simulation indicates the capability of DHGN to perform distributed multi-feature recognition on complex patterns, such as gray-scale images.

8.3   Distributed Data Management within Cloud Computing

Existing data management and access schemes in clouds are mainly based on Google File System (GFS) and MapReduce schemes. Problems arise when data are partitioned between numerous available nodes therein. A new method for partitioning and distributing data, known as resource virtualization in cloud computing, has been explored by Basirat et al. [56]. Loosely coupled associative computing techniques, which have not been commonly considered for clouds, can provide the required breakthrough for data management in Internet-scale infrastructures. Applications based on associative computing models can efficiently utilize the underlying hardware to dynamically scale up and down the system resources. In doing so, the main hurdle to providing scalable partitioning and distribution of data in clouds is removed, bringing forth a vastly superior solution for virtualizing data intensive applications and the system infrastructure to support the pay-per-use basis.

What is really required for any cloud system is a complete data access scheme that enables data partitioning on-the-fly and has the ability to disseminate processing nodes for specific data retrieval/storage tasks. A number of possibilities have been explored to consolidate the data access scheme using an efficient partitioning approach. This integration within a complete end-to-end scheme will enable data storage and retrieval processes to be performed effectively, regardless of the distribution of data within the cloud system. The aim is to develop a distributed data access scheme that enables data access to be conducted effectively by means of the distributed pattern recognition (DPR) approach. Data will be treated as a pattern, and data storage and retrieval will be performed through an unsupervised pattern recognition mechanism. This approach envisages data retrieval to be implemented as a distributed pattern recognition process that is implemented through the integration of loosely coupled computational networks. A divide-and-distribute approach allows for the dynamic distribution of these networks within the cloud.

8.3.1 Cloud Data Access Scheme

Data access schemes for a cloud infrastructure perform some important tasks, i.e., to administer a distribution of data across different networks and to provide data services for remote clients. In this section, we are going to discuss a cloud data access scheme using Google's MapReduce technique.

Google's MapReduce is a programming model intended for large-scale data processing in a massively parallel manner. It was developed to solve issues involving parallelization of computational processes and data distribution across heterogeneous networks. The MapReduce implementation also addresses load balancing, network performance, and fault tolerance issues [95].

The MapReduce programming model was inspired by other primitive languages, such as Lisp. It involves two functions: *map* and *reduce*. The map function is written by users and takes an input pair and produces a set of intermediate key/value pairs. Intermediate values associated with the same intermediate key are grouped by the MapReduce library and passed to the reduce function. The reduce function, also written by the user, merges all the intermediate values to form a possibly smaller set of values. Typically each invocation of the reduce function produces zero or one output.

Consider the following examples of map and reduce functions. Given a multiplication operation in a function $f(z)$, the following procedures illustrate both the map and reduce applications:

$$f(z) = map(\times 2, (2, 4, 6)) \rightarrow ((2 \times 2), (4 \times 2), (6 \times 2)) = (4, 8, 12)$$
$$f(z) = reduce(\times, (2, 4, 6)) \rightarrow ((2 \times 4) \times 6) = 48$$

Note that the map function is able to run the operation in parallel for all the inputs, whereas the reduce function works sequentially from left to right.

In the data access mechanism, the map and reduce functions are used to retrieve data from a collection of distributed repositories. The map function extracts the desired information based on a condition set by the user (it could be the condition within an SQL query). It works on the atomic level of data (a tuple or a file). The reduce function performs an operation on the data retrieved by the map function and obtains a set of values or a single value, as required by the user.

An important feature of MapReduce is its ability to parallelize the operations by working on each individual data and performing these tasks on-site. Consider the following example. Suppose there is a set of data related to employees' personal details, as shown in Table 8.3. An SQL query is performed to retrieve the average salary per department for executive employees as follows:

With this SQL query, MapReduce will conduct the map operation to obtain the name and salary amount of each employee in a department. Consequently, the reduce function will calculate the average salary according to each department. Figure 8.9 shows these operations.

Some problems arise in this type of processing configuration. For example, the map function conducts its operation assuming that data are distributed

---
Algorithm 5 SQL Query for Employee Data Example

1: Select E.deptName,
2:     Average(E.salaryAmt) as avgSalary
3: from Employee E
4: where P.status = Exec
5: groupby E.deptName

TABLE 8.3: Samples of Employee Data

employID	employFName	employLName	deptName	status	salaryAmt
00001	Robert	Harris	Admin	Exec	3000
00002	Mary	Richardson	HR	Non-Exec	2000
00003	Edward	Prack	Admin	Exec	3500
00004	Nancy	Ling	IT	Exec	3500
00005	Raj	Kumar	IT	Non-Exec	2000
00006	James	Harley	Finance	Exec	4000

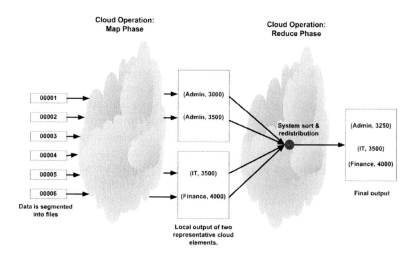

FIGURE 8.9: MapReduce implementation on a cloud system to determine the average executive salary for each department using the employee data in Table 8.3.

vertically, i.e., different records are distributed across the network. However, there are situations where some parts of the records are stored in different locations. For instance, a large database table is split into different sub-tables.

In addition, the operations of the MapReduce functions produce many intermediary entities between the map and reduce functions. These entities, as shown in Figure 8.9, are in the form of intermediate files. The contents of these files must be sorted before being fed to the reduce function. These system sorts and redistributions incur additional processing and communication costs.

In view of these issues, a data access scheme that enables retrieval to be conducted across multiple records and data segments in a single-cycle and parallel approach is considered. The access mechanism is implemented according to the nature of the database. The retrieval process will be conducted on a set of records that reside in a particular node. No alterations will be made to the condition of the record itself. A parallel retrieval approach is used, in which records in each storage node are analyzed locally without incurring any communication costs. A distributed pattern matching/recognition approach, such as the DHGN, can be used to retrieve data from the cloud.

8.3.2   DHGN Approach for Cloud Data Access

Through the redesign of the data management architecture, data records are treated as patterns. This treatment enables data storage and retrieval by association over and above the existing simple data referential mechanisms. Processing the database and handling the dynamic load is performed through a distributed pattern recognition approach that is implemented in integrated and loosely coupled computational networks and is followed by a divide-and-distribute approach that allows for the dynamic distribution of these networks within the cloud. The DHGN cloud access scheme relies on communications between adjacent nodes. The decentralized content location schemes are implemented to discover the adjacent nodes in a minimal number of hops. A GN-based algorithm for optimally distributing the DHGN subnets (clusters or sub-domains) across the cloud nodes is provided to automate the boot-strapping of the distributed application and to investigate dynamic load balancing over the network. Figure 8.10 shows how DHGN subnets are positioned in the cloud environment using a Hadoop's distributed file system (DFS) architecture.

Note that the DHGN subnets perform data mapping on each of the data nodes within the DFS infrastructure. Within each DHGN subnet, the records are stored in an associative pattern; each DHGN neuron corresponds to a single data field. The mapping process occurs within the body of the DHGN subnet. The SQL condition will activate the neuron that holds the respective data field. Figure 8.11 shows the data representation in the DHGN data access cloud scheme.

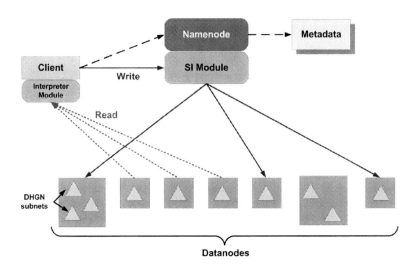

FIGURE 8.10: DHGN distributed data management model using the Hadoop DFS architecture.

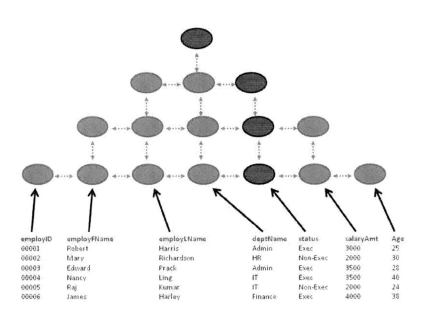

FIGURE 8.11: Data mapping process using a DHGN subnet as a repository, based on the pattern associative concept.

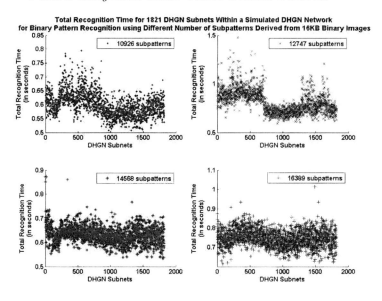

FIGURE 8.12: Total recognition times for each DHGN subnet in binary pattern recognition using different numbers of subpatterns derived from 16 KB binary images. ©IEEE. Reprinted, with permission, from Amin, A.H.M.; Khan, A.I.; "A divide-and-distribute approach to single-cycle learning HGN network for pattern recognition," Control Automation Robotics & Vision (ICARCV), 2010 11th International Conference on 7-10 Dec. 2010, pp. 2118-2123, doi: 10.1109/ICARCV.2010.5707852.

Note that the red-colored neurons are the query-activated neurons. The DHGN subnet will extract information from the database that pertains to the respective value specified in the query. In this example, the neuron that handles data on the status of the employee will select all of the tuples containing the *"exec"* status (see Algorithm 5).

The DHGN's pattern matching capability and the short response time remain insensitive to the increases in the number of stored patterns and make this approach ideal for cloud computing (see Figure 8.12). Moreover, the DHGN does not require rules to be defined, manual interventions by an operator to set thresholds to achieve the desired results, or heuristics entailing iterative operations for the memorization and recall of patterns [56]. In addition, this approach allows induction of new patterns in a fixed number of steps and maintains a high level of scalability, i.e., the performance and accuracy do not degrade as the number of stored pattern increases over time. Its pattern recognition capability is comparable with contemporary approaches. Furthermore, all computations are completed in the pre-defined number of steps, and thus the approach implements one shot, i.e., single-cycle learning.

8.4   Adaptive Recognition: A Different Perspective

In this chapter, we have presented a series of discussions on and examples of distributed pattern recognition (DPR) applications in coarse-grained computational networks. Network granularity is important when considering different types of Internet-scale data and applications. To achieve a scalable recognition scheme, we believe that such applications must be adaptive to different levels of network granularity. Recognition in the context of present time is not limited to complex data analysis, which runs on high-performance machines. Rather, we see the rapid development of lightweight devices that can perform complex operations, e.g., sensors, mobile phones, and any other wearable devices.

We have demonstrated the capabilities of a purely DPR scheme, such as the DHGN, to address two different application perspectives in a coarse-grained network, i.e., data recognition and management. Analyzing large-scale and complex data, such as images, is difficult without the availability of scalable recognition schemes that work in computational networks. The criticality of the information required, e.g., a medical analysis, adds to the importance of having a fast recognition scheme that can scale up with large amounts of data.

In addition to image recognition, distributed data management is considered to be a promising avenue for Internet-scale and distributed pattern recognition applications. Using a data association approach, it is believed that the DPR scheme can enhance the performance of existing data access schemes, such as MapReduce, which has been proven effective in the cloud environment.

In the next chapter, we will consider applications of Internet-scale pattern recognition in a different form of network, i.e., the fine-grained network.

Chapter 9

Event Detection within Fine-Grained Networks

The intensive development of wireless technologies and the increasing miniaturization of RF devices and micro electro-mechanical systems (MEMS) have been driving forces in the advancement of small and tiny computing devices, such as WSN technology. These devices are inter-connected and form a computational network that is capable of providing a frontline processing scheme for applications such as event detection and remote monitoring. Because this type of network has a large number of computing nodes that have limited power, storage, and processing capabilities, it is referred to as a fine-grained network.

The ability to acquire resource-awareness characteristics was discussed in the previous chapter and is essential for the design of distributed applications, including pattern recognition. The DHGN as a distributed pattern recognition scheme was developed with adaptive granularity characteristics built into its design. A distributed and parallel pattern recognition scheme for applications in fine-grained systems was introduced by Khan and Mihailescu [2].

In a fully distributed configuration, each GN is assigned to a single compute node, and the collaborations of inter-connected compute nodes form a DHGN subnet. The simple bias array search computations involved for each node make this configuration well-suited for fine-grained networks that have limited processing and storage capabilities, such as a WSN. We will demonstrate the robustness and scalability of the DHGN for a distributed recognition process over a fine-grained network using a number of DPR applications.

9.1 Distributed Event Detection Scheme for Wireless Sensor Networks

Highly complex computations, iterative learning, and large training set requirements are some of the weaknesses of event detection schemes commonly deployed in Wireless Sensor Networks (WSNs). These schemes often apply conventional neural networks or machine learning algorithms that require extensive retraining and a huge number of training data sets for effective generalization. Furthermore, the centralized processing or single-processing approach used in existing schemes creates some significant problems. For example, the constant flow of sensory data results in high communication overheads; rerouting procedures and relocation activities of sensor nodes that often occur in real-time applications; and significantly long delays in detecting critical events when computational bottlenecks are present. These problems limit the event detection schemes' ability to scale up to massive sensory data processing.

Artificial neural networks (ANNs) and other machine learning techniques are the most commonly applied classification techniques in event detection schemes for WSNs. Some of these schemes implement the Kohonen Self-Organizing Map (SOM) or other activation-based neural networks, such as the Radial Basis Function (RBF) neural network. Because of their learning complexity and highly cohesive training-validation approach, these schemes cannot scale up to the dynamics of the WSN network.

9.1.1   WSN Event Detection

Breakthroughs in communication technologies have enhanced the performance of existing coarse-grained networks, such as cloud and grid computing. Research has also led to the rapid growth of emerging fine-grained networks, such as wireless sensor networks (WSNs). These networks emerged from the confluence of wireless communication, extensive computational schemes, and sophisticated sensor technology. For example, WSNs are created from a collection of self-organized wireless and battery-powered devices that have sensing capabilities. The emergence of these self-organized networks of tiny processing devices has led to the ability for parallel and distributed computing deployment in fine-grained systems.

Unfortunately, the current scenario in WSN deployment is still far away from its tremendous potential. A WSN has only been demonstrated for humble applications such as meter reading in buildings and a basic form of ecological monitoring. Achieving the full potential of this technology requires the development of an intelligent computational scheme.

Common approaches implemented in existing WSN applications usually involve a number of processing steps, including sensory data capture and conveyance of these data to a central entity, known as the base station, for further refinement and analysis. Consequently, if it is called up for widespread use, this approach leads to a system bottleneck. Because of latency between the data capture/aggregation and processing time, processing delays occur intermittently. These limitations make WSNs less suitable for real-time monitoring applications. Therefore, a new approach for data processing in a WSN must be designed that has the ability to process the sensory data in situ and in a decentralized manner and can generate highly condensed and sophisticated outputs internally. These abilities alleviate the bottleneck problem in WSNs

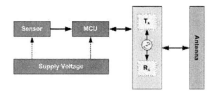

FIGURE 9.1: A generic wireless sensor node architecture. (This figure is a copyright of and reproduced with permission of Civil-Comp Ltd. Previously published in [96].)

TABLE 9.1: Berkeley Mica Mote Sensor Node Specifications

Component	Specification
CPU:	8-bit 4 MHz
Memory:	128 KB Flash and 4 KB RAM
Communication:	916 MHz 40 Kbps Radio
Power:	2 AA Batteries

(This table is a copyright of and reproduced with permission of Civil-Comp Ltd. Previously published in [96].)

using on-site computations, and they improve performance by reducing the processing delay experienced in existing approaches.

Figure 9.1 shows a generic wireless sensor node architecture. Currently, there are a number of commercially available wireless sensor nodes for different types of applications. These include the Berkeley Mica Mote *(http://www.xbow.com)* and the UCLA iBadge. The specifications of the Berkeley Mica Mote sensor node, which is used in a number of surveillance networks, are listed in Table 9.1.

On a macro level, a WSN is built up from a network of wireless sensor nodes that are linked together through a common entity, known as the base station or sink. Because of limited power and processing capabilities, communications between sensor nodes and the base station usually involve a series of data aggregation techniques to reduce the volume of traffic enroute to the base station.

9.1.2 DHGN-WSN Event Detection Configuration

In a fully distributed DHGN configuration, a collection of sensor nodes collaborate and form a DHGN subnet to perform event detection based on the sensory readings obtained from their environment. This is illustrated in Figure 9.2.

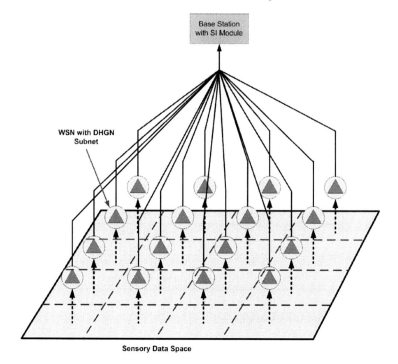

FIGURE 9.2: DHGN distributed event detection framework. (Muhamad Amin, A.H., Khan, A.I., and Raja Mahmood, R.A. "A distributed event detection scheme for wireless sensor networks," In Proceedings of the 7th International Conference on Advances in Mobile Computing and Multimedia (MoMM '09), pp. 295–299. ©2009 ACM, Inc. Reprinted by permission. http://doi.acm.org/10.1145/1821748.1821804)

Note that the SI module is intended to be deployed in a controlling node, such as the base station, or a super-node. The DHGN subnet module is located in each WSN subnet that is located within a specific sensory region. The event classification process (evaluation of event/non-event signals) in the DHGN event detection scheme is a dual-layer process. The first layer focuses on the subpattern recognition in the DHGN subnet, whereas the second layer involves pattern classification using a voting scheme that is conducted by the SI module. Subpattern recognition is the process of determining the recall/store status of an input subpattern. This process is conducted in DHGN subnets. The output of this process is either a recalled index of the stored subpattern or a new index for the input subpattern. This index is sent to the SI module for pattern classification. Note that the DHGN considers an event as a pattern that represents a state of normality or abnormality for the entire sensory network.

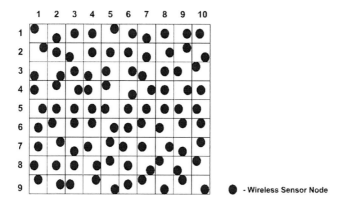

FIGURE 9.3: Sensor node placement in a Cartesian grid. Each node is allocated to a specific grid area. (This figure is copyright of and reproduced with permission of Civil-Comp Ltd. Previously published in [96].)

For complex event detection (multiple sensory schemes), each DHGN subnet is mapped to a sensor node using a clustered configuration. The detection scheme comprises a collection of wireless sensor nodes and a sink. We examine the deployment of the WSN in a two-dimensional plane with n sensors, represented by a set $W = (w_1, w_2, \ldots, w_n)$, where w_i denotes the ith sensor. The sensors are uniformly placed in a grid-like area, $A = (x \times y)$, where x represents the x-axis coordinate of the grid area, and y represents the y-axis coordinate of the grid area. Each sensor node is assigned to a specific grid area, as shown in Figure 9.3. The location of each sensor node is represented by the coordinates of its grid area (x_i, y_i).

For the communication model, a single-hop mechanism for data transmission from the sensor node to the sink is proposed. The *"autosend"* approach is used to minimize errors associated with the loss of packets during data transmission. Because of the front-end processing approach, the proposed scheme does not involve massive transmissions of sensor readings from the sensor nodes to the sink. Previous research has shown that the single-hop mechanism is the most suitable approach for the DHGN deployment. Communication between the sink and the sensor nodes is performed using a broadcast method.

9.1.3 Dimensionality Reduction in Sensory Data

Event detection involves the recognition of significant changes or abnormalities in sensory readings. In heterogeneous sensor networks, sensory readings are of different types and values, e.g., temperature, light intensity, and wind speed. In the DHGN implementation, these data must be pre-processed and transformed into an acceptable format while maintaining the values of the

TABLE 9.2: Examples of Simple Temperature Readings and Their Respective Binary Signature

Temperature Threshold Range (°C)	Binary Signature
0–20	10000
21–40	01000
41–60	00100
61–80	00010
81–100	00001

readings. As an example, to obtain a standardized format for the pattern input from various sensory readings, the use of an adaptive threshold binary signature scheme for dimensionality reduction and standardization is considered for multiple sensory data. The binary signature is a compact representation that is capable of representing different types of data with different values using a binary format [72]. Table 9.2 shows examples of temperature data ranges that have been converted into a series of binary signatures.

9.1.4 Event Classification

The DHGN distributed event detection scheme involves a bottom-up classification technique, in which the classification of events is determined from the sensory readings obtained through the WSN. The approach pre-processes patterns using dimensionality reduction techniques, such as the adaptive threshold binary signature scheme. These patterns are propagated to all available DHGN subnets for recognition and classification purposes.

The recognition process involves finding dissimilarities between the input patterns and previously stored patterns. Any dissimilar patterns will create a response for further analysis, whereas similar patterns will be recalled. This research used the supervised single-cycle learning approach in a DHGN to perform recognition based on the stored patterns. The stored patterns in our proposed scheme include the set of ordinary events that are translated into normal surrounding/environmental conditions. These patterns are derived from the results of an analysis conducted at the base station, which is based on the continuous feedback from the sensor nodes. Figure 9.4 shows the workflow for the distributed event detection.

The event detection scheme using the DHGN incorporates twos levels of recognition: front-end recognition and back-end recognition. Front-end recognition involves using the DHGN pattern matching mechanism to determine if the sensor readings obtained by the sensor nodes indicate an extraordinary event or a normal surrounding condition. Conversely, the spatial occurrence detection is conducted through the back-end recognition. In this approach, the use of signals sent by sensor nodes is considered to be a pattern for detecting event occurrences in a specific area or location.

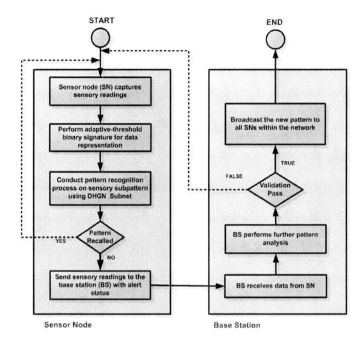

FIGURE 9.4: A process workflow for the DHGN distributed event detection in a WSN. (This figure is a copyright of and reproduced with permission of Civil-Comp Ltd. Previously published in [96].)

9.1.4.1 Pattern Matching at Sensory Level

The occurrences of abnormal events are detected using a pattern matching approach. Sensory readings are considered to be patterns, and any significant changes in the structure of normal patterns are classified as events or critical events that must be reported back to the sink (or other master node). The use of a clustered DHGN configuration maps each sensor node with a DHGN subnet that is able to accept a number of different sensory readings as a single subpattern. The following algorithm describes our proposed pattern matching approach for event detection at the sensor level.

In this algorithm, the output of the pattern matching process is a signal, which alerts the SI module of the detection of a new event. The base station will respond by performing a spatio-temporal analysis on the readings obtained.

9.1.5 Performance Metrics: Memory Utilization

Memory utilization estimation for the DHGN algorithm involves an analysis of the bias array capacity for all of the GNs in the distributed architecture

---

Algorithm 6 Pattern Matching Function at the Sensor Level

1: given n sensory readings for time t: $S_t = (s_1, s_2, ...s_n)$
2: convert S_t to a binary signature B_t. Therefore $f(binsig) : S_t \mapsto B_t$
3: $trigger = FALSE$
4: $eventAlert.Sensor = FALSE$
5: **repeat**
6:   **for** $i = 0$ to $MAXREADINGS$ **do**
7:     {check for matched subpatterns (sensory readings) in sensor data storage}
8:     **if** $new.B_t == s[i].Sensor$ **then**
9:       {$new.B_t$: new readings, matching process is conducted using the DHGN algorithm}
10:       exit FOR
11:     **else**
12:       $s[MAXREADINGS + 1].Sensor = new.B_t$
13:       $trigger = TRUE$
14:       $eventAlert.Sensor = TRUE$
15:     **end if**
16:   **end for**
17: **until** $trigger = TRUE$
18: send $eventAlert.Sensor$ and $s[MAXREADINGS+1].Sensor$ to SI module function at base station
19: $MAXREADINGS = MAXREADINGS + 1$

---

and the storage capacity of the SI module node. A detailed analysis of the bias array capacity for the GN-based algorithm was presented in Chapter 3. Based on that analysis, it can be concluded that the efficient storage/recall mechanism of the DHGN offers efficient memory utilization. Furthermore, it only uses memory to store newly discovered patterns rather than storing all pattern inputs. Figure 9.5 compares the estimated memory capacities for a DHGN processing cluster to the maximum memory size of a typical physical senor node (Table 9.1) as a function of the subpattern size.

As shown in the Figure 9.5, as the size of subpattern increases, the memory space requirement increases considerably. Note that the small subpattern sizes consume less than 1% of the total memory space available. Therefore, the DHGN implementation is best deployed for small subpattern sizes.

9.1.6 Spatio-Temporal Analysis of Event Data

The spatio-temporal analysis is a process of observing the frequency and distribution of events within the wireless sensor networks. It is conducted at the base station with computational grid-enabled infrastructure, since it has the bird's eye view of the overall network. An analysis on forest fire detection

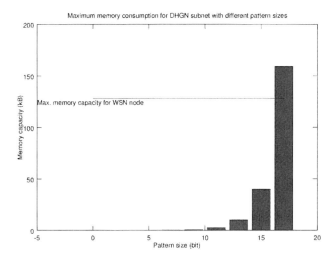

FIGURE 9.5: Maximum memory consumption for each DHGN subnet as a function of the pattern size. The DHGN uses minimal memory space when processing small pattern sizes.

by including a spatio-temporal consideration has been reported in [96]. In this work, pattern recognition was performed on the overall responses from the wireless sensor nodes obtained. In this context, the signals sent by each sensor node will colectively form a spatio-temporal representation in the form of spatial coordinates and time instances. The detection area used in this analysis is represented in the form of Cartesian coordinates with the grid size of 9×5 obtained from the data set in [97]. Figure 9.6 shows a scenario of spatio-temporal analysis using the proposed scheme.

Note the changes in the distribution of event across different geographical coordinates over 25 time instances (*t01* to *t25*). Note that the light-shaded area represents the area in which forest fire was detected using the allocated wireless sensor node with DHGN scheme, while dark-shaded area represents the area in which its sensor node responses with non-event signal. The non-shaded area represents area with no active node at the respective time instances.

This capability of deploying spatio-temporal event detection opens up further possibility for enhanced event detection mechanism capable of providing measures on the distribution of events over a specified time period. Furthermore, simple event tracking approach may be performed by examining the order of magnitude and the direction of the occurrences of events, as shown in Figure 9.7.

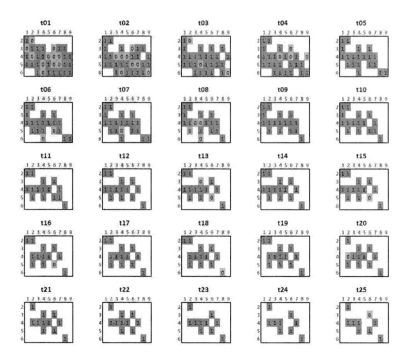

FIGURE 9.6: Spatio-temporal view of the forest fire distribution across the affected area, which is represented in the form of Cartesian coordinates. (This figure is a copyright of and reproduced with permission of Civil-Comp Ltd. Previously published in [96].)

9.2 Integrated Grid-Sensor Scheme for Structural Analysis

The development of state-of-the-art structures has led to a requirement for efficient structural health monitoring and management (SHM). Sophisticated structures, such as aerospace vehicles, offshore oil and gas structures, military maritime vehicles, and intelligent buildings, require continuous and rapid health analysis, design, and monitoring. These activities are essential to ensuring the optimal operational performance of such critical structures. Furthermore, these structures are highly invested and incur extremely high replacement costs. SHM involves continuous processes of analyzing, designing, and monitoring structures. These processes are important in obtaining the up-to-date status of the structures and maintaining their performance. Several approaches have been considered by engineering practices. These include the

Time Progression, t

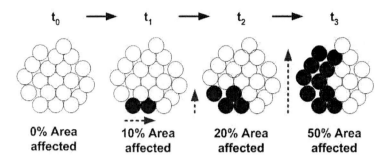

FIGURE 9.7: Analysis of event data triggered by the sensor nodes and received by the base station. (Muhamad Amin, A.H., Khan, A.I., and Raja Mahmood, R.A. "A distributed event detection scheme for wireless sensor networks," In Proceedings of the 7th International Conference on Advances in Mobile Computing and Multimedia (MoMM '09), pp. 295–299. ©2009 ACM, Inc. Reprinted by permission. http://doi.acm.org/10.1145/1821748.1821804)

use of wireless sensor network (WSN) technology in SHM, which enables the analysis and monitoring to be conducted in real time. The sensors are built-in to monitor the state of the structures and provide instantaneous feedback.

In this section, we outline a full-scale SHM framework that adopts wireless sensors and grid integration. It allows for complete structural analysis, design, and monitoring to be conducted within the design and monitoring life cycle and in a single processing environment. This integrated grid-sensor framework is a combination of WSNs for data recognition and a collection of commodity-grid based processors for large-scale structural data analysis. The proposed framework implements an in-network processing, or compressed sensing, scheme known as Graph Neuron (GN), which enables real-time monitoring in resource constrained sensor networks. With suitable extension, GN can also be deployed in grid-enabled environments. This approach allows for multi-level data analysis and monitoring to be conducted in the SHM framework.

The SHM framework encompasses several processes that work in a cyclic manner. In keeping with a holistic framework for the structural engineering processes, the required processes will be conducted within a single life cycle. The life cycle is characterized by three main processes: structural analysis, structural design, and structural monitoring. These processes are inter-related, as shown in Figure 9.8.

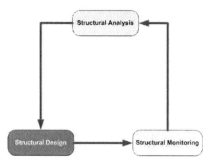

FIGURE 9.8: Structural design and monitoring life cycle.

9.2.1 Integrated Grid-Sensor Network Framework for Structural Engineering

The integrated grid-sensor network framework for structural engineering embeds both grid computing environments for parallel adaptive finite element analysis (FEA) and WSNs for SHM. The framework offers seamless analysis, design, and monitoring for structural health within a single life cycle. This approach introduces a new level of sophistication into the management of complex and often very expensive engineering structures. Furthermore, the combination of real-life information obtained from the sensors and the theoretical structure information developed using finite element analysis can lead to further economies in the structural design. The integrated framework combines a WSN and a grid environment in a single architectural platform. This framework enables the structural analyses to be farmed out to the computational grid community and provides continuous monitoring for such analyses (and other SHM applications) using a WSN. This framework requires an adaptive system architecture that is able to provide real-time or near real-time communication between the WSN and the computational grid. Furthermore, rapid structural analysis, design, and monitoring require fast processing with large storage capacity for storing real-time structural information generated by the network. These requirements can be delivered using existing computational grid technology, such as the commodity grid described in Section 8.1.2.

The system architecture for this integrated framework implements a commodity grid and a high-speed WSN-to-grid network. Figure 9.9 presents this architecture.

The computational grid for this framework also takes into account the data storage capability, as shown in this figure. Note that the grid environment can be further extended to include multiple compute grids. In addition, grid proxy is implemented to ensure that other WSN networks are able to utilize the grid for their structural health analysis and design. Therefore, this framework can act as a shared commodity for the entire structural engineering community.

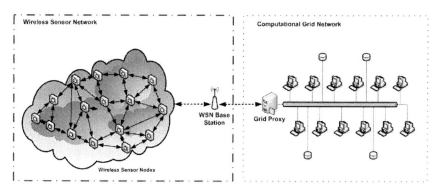

FIGURE 9.9: Conceptual system architecture for the proposed integrated grid-sensor network framework for the structural engineering life cycle.

9.2.2 Structural Analysis, Design, and Monitoring Applications

There are three specific applications for the integrated grid-sensor network framework in a structural engineering life cycle: structural pattern matching within a WSN, parallel adaptive FEA, and grid-enabled pattern recognition for the feedback and data integrity analysis. These applications are incorporated in a single grid workflow, as shown in Figure 9.10.

9.2.2.1 One-Shot Structural Pattern Matching in a Sensor Network

Adaptive FEA [99] provides the means to predict the behavior of a range of electromechanical and structural systems that are under the influence of anticipated load conditions accurately. These analyses are heavily relied on in complex engineering designs. Meaningful information can be derived by correlating the input patterns, gathered *in situ* by a WSN, with the patterns calculated by an FEA using the latent associative memory of the network. Because the associative memory must be implemented in a network that has very limited computational resources, the governing algorithm must be modified to suit the limitations of the operating environment. This would generally entail the replacement of complex sequential algorithms with parallel/decentralized algorithms. Moreover, some drop in the accuracy of pattern matching might occur, which could be offset by further processing at the remote system's end (WSN base station). To provide an accurate pattern matching scheme and simultaneously reduce the computational requirements in resource-restricted networks while provide responses in real time, a GN algorithm is considered.

The GN approach (see Section 3.1) models the parallelism available in naturally occurring associative memory (AM) systems and bypasses the deficiencies present in some contemporary approaches. The GN is implemented

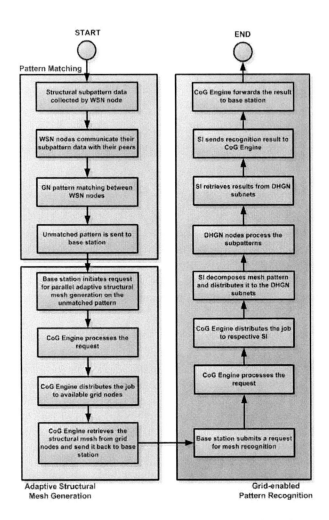

FIGURE 9.10: Workflow for the proposed integrated grid-sensor network framework. (This figure is a copyright of and reproduced with permission of Civil-Comp Ltd. Previously published in [98].)

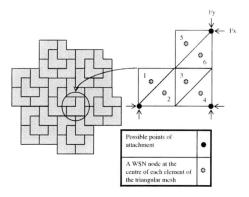

FIGURE 9.11: A continuum of L-shaped plates with embedded WSNs. (This figure is a copyright of and reproduced with permission of Civil-Comp Ltd. Previously published in [98].)

as a self-organizing (ad hoc) virtual network of processing nodes. Each node executes the same copy of a very simple AM algorithm, which provides a natural framework for supporting parallelism. The algorithm is best suited for immensely parallel systems, such as WSNs.

9.2.2.1.1 GN for stress pattern detection in a WSN In SHM, an arbitrary L-shaped plate with in-plane loading is used as an object of investigation. It is assumed that each of these plates is embedded with a WSN, as shown in Figure 9.11.

Complex shapes can be formed using these simple L-shaped plates. The embedded WSN can measure strain, stress, displacement, or any other parameter of importance in the design of this continuum. These parameters are assumed to be vectors orthogonal to the plane of the WSN. The in-plane stresses have been selected as the orthogonal vector for this study. Two stress states, of the six possible states under the horizontal and vertical load conditions, were arbitrarily selected to demonstrate the in-network pattern recognition capability of the application. It is assumed that these two stress patterns are highly detrimental to the continuum and must be watched so that their occurrences are detected in real time. These patterns can result for non-critical stress states. However, the final determination of the pattern detected by the WSN is performed outside of the network, where greater computational resources can be made available for interpolating stress readings obtained from a relatively coarse-grained WSN.

9.2.2.2 Parallel Adaptive Mesh Refinement

The patterns picked up by the WSN through in-network processing can only represent binary level variations in the patterns. It is possible that the pattern detected is not the critical pattern. In addition, these patterns represent a very coarse sample comprising relatively few readings. Therefore, WSN node readings (in each pre-selected sample) must be compared with the critical patterns. Adaptive mesh refinement provides a well-adjusted finite element mesh, which can be used for interpolating the values at a finer scale. The interpolated values can be readily compared with the critical pattern values. This would verify if the critical pattern was indeed encountered in one or more of the WSNs.

To develop the finite element mesh, we propose a parallel processing approach to finite element mesh generation that harnesses the capability of computational grid networks to process large-scale data. We propose a parallel adaptive finite element mesh generated using a Domain Decomposition (DD) concept. In Domain Decomposition, a domain of interest is decomposed into multiple sub-domains. Each sub-domain is delegated to a single processing node in the computational grid network.

9.2.2.2.1   Adaptive finite element analysis   The state of the mechanical, structural, and electrical components may be effectively modeled using the well-established numerical technique, adaptive FEA. A stress-strain based finite element model was selected to distinguish between the various stress states. To achieve a finite element solution that is close to the actual response of the material, it can be assumed that the continuum is idealized using a large number of elements. The size of each element is very small in comparison to the dimensions of the continuum. Therefore, the actual element stresses will tend to be constant over each of the elements, and the solution can be regarded as accurate for all practical purposes. However, doing so requires the use of a very fine mesh. To avoid the computational cost associated with a very fine mesh, an adaptive refinement of the mesh is carried out.

Figure 9.12 provides a detailed distribution of stresses over the L-plate from the previous sub-section. However, the values obtained from the WSN will only provide the readings at the center of each of the six WSN nodes embedded in the plate. The values at other points in the WSN must be estimated using an interpolation scheme that can refine the values measured by the sparse set of WSN nodes to a continuum.

9.2.2.2.2   Parallel approach to finite element mesh generation   Finite element analysis is considered to be a purely sequential approach for mesh generation. However, several studies have parallelized this approach. These studies include the works by Jimack and Nadeem [100] on the parallel domain decomposition algorithm for adaptive finite element solution of three-dimensional convection-diffusion problems; and Fragakis and Onate [101] in their work on parallel Delaunay triangulation for particle finite element methods. To generate the mesh for the L-plated surface in the previous sub-sections, we implemented a geometric decomposition of the surface, as shown in Figure

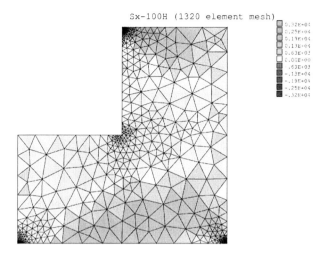

FIGURE 9.12: An iteratively refined adaptive finite element discretization showing the distribution of the horizontal loading. (This figure is a copyright of and reproduced with permission of Civil-Comp Ltd. Previously published in [98].)

9.13. Note that each sub-surface is assigned to a specific processing node in the grid.

Once the mesh is generated from the initial structural pattern obtained from the GN pattern matching scheme, the next procedure in our integrated grid-sensor network framework is the pattern recognition process involving the meshes (both normal and damaged structural patterns).

9.2.2.3 DPR Scheme for Damage Detection Using Mesh Representation

To provide a continuous measure in structural analysis, design, and monitoring, we propose a second-level recognition for the structural pattern. At this level, the recognition process involves the recognition of a damaged structural mesh representation using the stored meshes of normal structural conditions. The meshes generated from the previous stage of the framework are treated as images, and a distributed image recognition scheme, such as the DHGN, is deployed.

Using the sub-domain meshes generated from the parallel adaptive finite element mesh generation, we compare the meshes obtained from the WSN network with the pre-stored meshes in the computational grid network. Figure 9.14 shows a simple mesh recognition process using the DHGN approach.

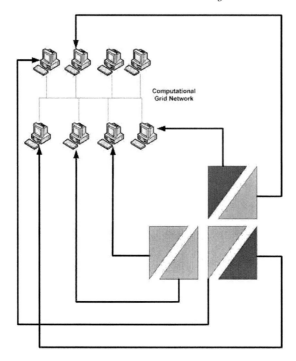

FIGURE 9.13: Geometric decomposition of the L-shaped surface for vertical load conditions. Note that each sub-surface is assigned to a single processing node in the grid. (This figure is a copyright of and reproduced with permission of Civil-Comp Ltd. Previously published in [98].)

By distributing the recognition process on sub-domain meshes, the recognition time and complexity are minimized, and solutions can be provided in real or near real time. This distributed recognition scheme is able to enhance the integrated framework and deliver a real time solution for new types of structures.

9.3   Distributed Event Detection: A Lightweight Approach

In this chapter, two distributed pattern recognition applications in a fine-grained system were presented: distributed event detection in a WSN and an integrated sensor-grid framework for structural health monitoring (SHM). These examples demonstrated the capabilities of DPR algorithms, such as the DHGN and GN, to perform a distributed and lightweight detection mechanism

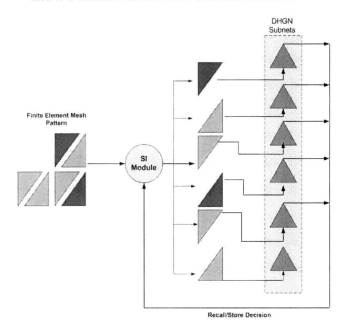

FIGURE 9.14: Damage detection using the DHGN distributed pattern recognition scheme. (This figure is a copyright of and reproduced with permission of Civil-Comp Ltd. Previously published in [98].)

for event occurrences in a resource-constrained network, such as a WSN. There are several benefits to the DPR implementation. The distributed approach uses a simple bias array representation that offers low memory consumption for event data storage. Furthermore, the recognition scheme only stores subpatterns/patterns that relate to normal events rather than keeping the records of all occurring events. This work also demonstrated that this new approach is most effective for small subpattern sizes because it uses only a small portion of the memory space of a typical physical sensor node in a WSN. In addition to this efficient memory usage, DPR schemes, such as the DHGN, eliminate the need for complex computations for event classification techniques. With the adoption of single-cycle learning and adjacency comparison approaches, the DHGN implements non-iterative and lightweight computational mechanisms for event recognition and classification. The distributed characteristic of the DHGN implies that it is readily deployable over a distributed network. With such features, the DHGN can perform as a front-end detection scheme for event detection in a WSN. Through a divide-and-distribute approach, complex events are perceived as a composition of events occurring at a specific time and location. By incorporating a spatio-temporal evaluation of events, this new approach would be able to be used in event tracking in the future.

Part V

The Way Forward

Chapter 10

Recognition: The Future and Beyond

"I have an almost religious zeal — not for technology per se, but for the Internet, which is for me the nervous system of mother Earth, which I see as a living creature, linking up." — **Dan Millman**

10.1 Medium of Change

Through the evolution of time, we can see how a simple electronic calculator has superseded the abacus, which was devised by people in the pre-historic era thousands of years ago. The functionalities of both devices are similar, i.e., a tool for arithmetic calculations. Currently, the use of the electronic calculator has reached far beyond the capabilities and functionalities of its predecessors while preserving its basic set of operations. Complex numerical calculations can be performed using existing scientific calculators that are available in the market.

The reason for starting the final chapter with this example is that we can see that improvements of functionality can be expected from changes that have been made to a device or object that is being used. As has once been said by Marshall McLuhan [127], *"A change of medium inevitably leads to a change in the message."* From this perspective, in regards to pattern recognition, we could argue that changes in the way we perform recognition might extend its functions and capabilities. This is relevant to the discussions that have been presented in this book. The way we look at how pattern recognition is performed can be changed if we consider a different approach, i.e., a distributed approach.

This book has been dedicated to exploring different ways of implementing pattern recognition using machine intelligence. Decades of work in improving pattern recognition algorithms have reached their height. It is now the time for us to revisit the fundamentals of biological intelligence, specifically human intelligence. As was mentioned in the preface of this book, the human brain is, in its actual form, a fully distributed network of computational machines, known as neurons. If we are able to map this into existing computational networks, we see that the Internet is actually a physical brain of our entire computational systems. Just as described in the quote by Dan Millman that opens this chapter. The question that remains to be considered is how we can harvest the functionalities of such large-scale systems. This perhaps can be solved by having computational schemes that work at Internet-scale.

10.2   Future of Internet-Scale PR

Pattern recognition has and will always be a part of our lives. For several decades, we have put much effort into delegating the recognition process to machines, specifically computers. The evolution of computing fields, such as robotics and machine learning, has provided a significant edge in enhancing the applications involving pattern recognition. In the future, we foresee that these applications will be extended beyond a simple domain-specific problem. We may need to take a step and look at the context of collaborative inter-domains. In addition, the recognition process can be applied beyond simple textual and numerical data. Rather, it can also be applied on the semantics of data. Current technological developments under the label of Internet-of-Things (IoT) [7] and System-of-Systems (SoS) [102] are making it possible to work from the perspective of collaborative inter-domains.

In today's common enterprises and industries, monitoring and controlling large-scale process control systems are important. The information systems designed for such applications require interoperability between heterogeneous distributed systems ranging from control networks to enterprise networks. The significance of the systems interoperability can be observed in industrial scenarios such as the plant lubrication system, where engineering, control, monitoring, and maintenance systems are interoperable and require perfect coordination for the system to perform its functions. In teaching systems, student information systems and examination systems can be integrated to create an automation of student's examination results and suggestions on possible course loads to be taken in the future. Although different types of systems are targeted to achieve a common goal in a particular industry or business, existing practices seem to be designed as silos, where the tyranny of manual actions are required to reach interoperability throughout the system. This type of approach is prone to human errors and is an unnecessary waste of resources. A complete integration and automation system that performs cross-layer operations between different systems within a single large-scale system, known as System of Systems (SoS), has a vast potential for solving these types of problems. With this approach being developed, it is important that each component system can dynamically be discovered, added, or removed. Furthermore, information exchange can be performed seamlessly between different systems, acting as a single large-scale ecosystem.

The Internet-of-Things (IoT) and System-of-Systems (SoS) have the potentials to provide the industry with imminence solutions for integrating and automating large-scale heterogeneous systems. For instance, in plant maintenance, data captured from the sensors and field devices can be transmitted immediately to the processing network and be made directly available to the plant engineer for analysis, trigger a request for parts procurement to the finance department, or trigger a delivery request to the warehouse manager. Although conceptually this approach offers significant added-value to the day-to-day operations of industries and enterprises, there remains a gap between theory and practice that lies at the knowledge level.

With the advent of IoT and SoS models, fully connected environments are possible. However, the knowledge potentials of high-connectivity between heterogeneous systems in a large-scale ecosystem must be extensively explored. For example, studies on cause and effect relationships can be extended to include different elements and parameters. Questions such as whether the flooding of a road or a road accident will impact a household's electricity usage or whether the rapid increase of temperature in a boiler room of a plant will reduce the duration of the procurement process. These questions will definitely be frowned upon because they not a part of the normal human experience. Nevertheless, an increased interconnectivity achieved through both IoT and SoS models have the potential to make such questions a reality. In the future, the aims are to discover the knowledge potentials of infrastructures that are able to add value to the way interpretations and analysis can be accomplished in our daily life's operations. This can only be achieved using distributed pattern recognition and analysis schemes when addressing such an Internet-scale environment.

Developing a capability for large-scale recognition and interpretation schemes based on both IoT and SoS models will require a detailed understanding of the complex relationship between the devices and information systems at a bigger scale. A set of accurate recognition models must be formulated to follow as real systems. This is to provide reasonable approximations of the resultant behavior. In this perspective, the level of sophistication required in knowledge of the occurrences of event will be of higher level than what is currently required, e.g., in weather prediction applications.

10.3 Making a Case

A case for Internet-scale pattern recognition has been made through the design and implementation of DPR, which has been extensively described in this book. Recognition by means of computational intelligence can no longer be established simply on the basis of algorithmic accuracy and efficiency. The context of scalability must also be considered. Existing demand for large-scale analyses can only be addressed using the enormous capacity of computational networks. In addition, a scheme for scalable and fully distributed pattern recognition is important because it will eliminate the implementation bottle-neck of existing tightly coupled and highly iterative recognition algorithms. Through these two mediums of change, pattern recognition can be used far beyond its existing capabilities.

As previously discussed in Chapter 1, we believe that the means for ex-isting artificial intelligence to emulate the functions of the human brain and nervous system is through connectivity. Having a fully distributed approach for information processing enables more information to be stored, and the ca-pacity to process such information is significantly increased. With the advent of seamless interconnectivity between smart devices, such as in the Internet-of-Things (IoT), this capability for large-scale data processing can be further extended. Furthermore, sensors attached to these large-scale computational networks will provide an avenue for real-time information processing with a life-long learning capability.

Imagine a fully interconnected sensory system composed of wireless sen-sors and a distributed recognition algorithm that could learn how events are happening and how it could adapt to any changes experienced throughout its lifetime, i.e., as a pseudo-conscious system that acts as humans do, avoiding hurtful situations using past experiences.

In the perspective of network evolution, we can see from the discussions in later chapters of this book that computational networks have evolved from a simple local network to computing at tera- or peta-flop scale. Cloud computing enables a highly scalable means for complex computations and promises enor-mous resource availability. In addition, the granularity of computational net-works has evolved from coarse-grained systems, such as a grid, to fine-grained networks, such as WSNs. The question that remains to be answered is how we can fully utilize such systems. This perhaps can only be answered if we are able to change our perspective of computations from sequential Von Neumann principles to a fully parallel and distributed computing approach. A paradigm shift is required, from Von Neumann archetype of stored-program computer to a purely in-network processing approach, in which computations can be performed in parallel within the body of the network without experiencing performance bottlenecks resulting from sequential instruction execution and data operations.

In the following subsections, we will look at the contributions of this book from two perspectives: the fundamentals of the recognition process and the idea of pattern recognition as a scalable commodity for information processing.

10.3.1   Changing the Fundamentals

For almost six decades, research on neural networks has focused on the learning functions to improve the accuracy and efficiency of neuron outputs.

Less attention has been paid to the aspect of neuron connectivity in the network. On this perspective, we can see a number of significant improvements in the accuracy of conventional pattern recognition schemes, such as Hopfield network. Nevertheless, the synaptic plasticity effect of tightly coupled learning algorithms, such as Hebbian learning, limits the scalability of these schemes. In relation to pattern recognition, to move beyond the boundaries of Internet-scale environments, it is important for us to revisit the fundamentals of neural networks. Throughout the discussions presented in this book, several important concepts of in-network processing for pattern recognition were presented. These included one-shot learning (Chapter 3), the hierarchical processing model (Chapter 4), and the divide-and-distribute approach (Chapter 5). These concepts build up the foundations of a DPR approach for Internet-scale recognition.

With the ability to expand recognition beyond the sequential train-validation-test approach of existing pattern recognition schemes, DPR enables recognition processes to be performed in a parallel and distributed manner. The distributed multi-feature recognition approach, discussed in Chapter 7, provides a scalable means of implementing recognition procedures on multiple data features. With the expanding network resource availability, one is capable of implementing pattern recognition using an unlimited number of features. This factor is important, as we can see from the McGurk effect [103], because certain features can be retrieved or detected only by using a combination of features. Instead of identifying information, we are able to generate information using distributed information processing.

10.3.2 Recognition as Commodity

Apart from changing the perspective of recognition, this book was also intended to deliver the concept of pattern recognition as a commodity for information processing applications. As was demonstrated in Chapters 8 and 9, DPR schemes, such as the DHGN, can be deployed in different types of computational networks. This adaptive feature for network granularity enables recognition processes to be treated as a generic service or commodity for different types of applications. We have demonstrated the use of DPR in face recognition and distributed event detection. The unique approach of the recognition process via in-network computations allows recognition to be performed regardless of the types of data being used. Thus, this approach enhances the scalability of the pattern recognition approach by taking into account the structure and resources available in a particular network.

With this concept of recognition as a commodity, we are able to fully utilize current and future technology, such as cloud computing, which has been developed with a service-oriented architecture (SOA). We can conceptualize pattern recognition as a cloud service that can be deployed in different types of analytical and information processing applications ranging from a simple image finder to complex analytical processes, such as protein structure analysis in bioinformatics.

Bibliography

[1] A. I. Khan, "A peer-to-peer associative memory network for intelligent information systems," in *Enabling Organisations and Society Through Information Systems: The Proceedings of The Thirteenth Australasian Conference on Information Systems, Melbourne, Victoria, Australia*, pp. 317–326, 2002.

[2] A. I. Khan and P. Mihailescu, "Parallel pattern recognition computations within a wireless sensor network," in *ICPR (1)*, pp. 777–780, 2004.

[3] B. B. Nasution and A. I. Khan, "A hierarchical graph neuron scheme for real-time pattern recognition," *IEEE Transactions on Neural Networks*, vol. 19, no. 2, pp. 212–229, 2008.

[4] A. Muhamad Amin and A. I. Khan, "Single-cycle image recognition using an adaptive granularity associative memory network," in *AI 2008: Advances in Artificial Intelligence*, (Berlin/Heidelberg), pp. 386–392, Springer, 2008. Accessed October 6, 2010.

[5] M. J. Watkins and J. M. Gardiner, "An appreciation of generate-recognize theory of recall," *Journal of Verbal Learning and Verbal Behavior*, vol. 18, no. 6, pp. 687–704, 1979.

[6] C. Kamath and R. Musick, "Scalable data mining through fine-grained parallelism: The present and the future," *Advances in Distributed and Parallel Knowledge Discovery*, pp. 29–77, 2000.

[7] H. Kopetz, "Internet of things," in *Real-Time Systems*, Real-Time Systems Series, pp. 307–323, Springer US, 2011.

[8] F. Rosenblatt, "The perceptron — a perceiving and recognizing automaton," *Technical Report No.85-460-1*, 1957.

[9] A. K. Jain, R. P. Duin, and J. Mao, "Statistical pattern recognition: A review," *IEEE Transactions on Pattern Analysis and Machine Intelligence*, vol. 22, no. 1, pp. 4–37, 2000.

[10] D. O. Hebb, "The organization of behavior," *Neurocomputing: Foundations of Research*, pp. 43–54, 1988.

[11] J. C. Schlimmer and R. H. Granger, Jr., "Incremental learning from noisy data," *Machine Learning*, vol. 1, no. 3, pp. 317–354, 1986.

[12] N. Nilsson, "Introduction to machine learning: An early draft of a proposed textbook," 1996. Accessed October 6, 2010.

[13] H. Sulehria and Y. Zhang, "Study on the capacity of hopfield neural networks," *Information Technology Journal*, vol. 7, no. 4, pp. 684–688, 2008.

[14] C. Anderson, "The end of theory: The data deluge makes the scientific method obsolete," 2008. Accessed March 3, 2010.

[15] S. K. Pal and P. Mitra, *Pattern Recognition Algorithms for Data Mining: Scalability, Knowledge Discovery, and Soft Granular Computing.* London, UK: Chapman & Hall, Ltd., 2004.

[16] J. Cheng and K. Wang, "Active learning for image retrieval with co-svm," *Pattern Recognition*, vol. 40, no. 1, pp. 330–334, 2007.

[17] G. Xia, Z. Tang, Y. Li, and J. Wang, "A binary hopfield neural network with hysteresis for large crossbar packet-switches," *Neurocomputing*, vol. 67, pp. 417–425, 2005.

[18] S.-J. Hsiao, W.-T. Sung, and K.-C. Fan, "Web-based distributed pattern recognition system," *Information Visualisation, International Conference on*, p. 375, 2002.

[19] Y. Guoqing, C. Songcan, and L. Jun, "Multilayer parallel distributed pattern recognition system model using sparse ram nets," *Computers and Digital Techniques, IEEE Proceedings on*, vol. 139, pp. 144–146, Mar 1992.

[20] G. Nagy, "Interactive, mobile, distributed pattern recognition," in *CIAP05*, pp. 37–49, 2005.

[21] H. Al-Hertani and J. Ilow, "Pattern recognition based detection and localization in a network of randomly distributed sensor nodes," in *ISDA '05: Proceedings of the 5th International Conference on Intelligent Systems Design and Applications*, (Washington, DC, USA), pp. 412–419, IEEE Computer Society, 2005.

[22] H.-C. Choi and S.-Y. Oh, "Efficient human-like memory management based on walsh-based associative memory for real-time pattern recognition," in *IJCNN*, pp. 3657–3663, 2006.

[23] A. Talukder, T. Sheikh, and L. Chandramouli, "Real-time intelligent pattern recognition, resource management and control under constrained resources for distributed sensor networks," *Neural Networks, IEEE Proceedings International Joint Conference on*, vol. 2, pp. 1321–1326, July 2004.

[24] I. Turkoglu and A. Arslan, "Optimisation of the performance of neural network based pattern recognition classifiers with distributed sys-

tems," *Parallel and Distributed Systems ICPADS 2001, Proceedings of the Eighth International Conference on*, pp. 379–382, 2001.

[25] G. Garai and B. Chaudhuri, "A distributed hierarchical genetic algorithm for efficient optimization and pattern matching," *Pattern Recognition*, vol. 40, no. 1, pp. 212–228, 2007.

[26] A. V. Srinivas and D. Janakiram, "A model for characterizing the scalability of distributed systems," *SIGOPS Oper. Syst. Rev.*, vol. 39, no. 3, pp. 64–71, 2005.

[27] J. Hopfield and D. Tank, "Neural computation of decisions in optimization problems," *Biological Cybernetics*, vol. 52, pp. 141–152, 1985.

[28] G. Ritter and P. Sussner, "An introduction to morphological neural networks," *Pattern Recognition, International Conference on*, vol. 4, pp. 709–717, 1996.

[29] M. Hassoun and P. Watta, "The hamming associative memory and its relation to the exponential capacity dam," in *Neural Networks, 1996, IEEE International Conference on*, vol. 1, pp. 583–587, June 1996.

[30] T. Kohonen, *Self-Organizing Maps*. Springer, 3rd ed., December 2000.

[31] A. I. Khan, M. Isreb, and R. S. Spindler, "A parallel distributed application of the wireless sensor network," in *HPCASIA '04: Proceedings of the High Performance Computing and Grid in Asia Pacific Region, Seventh International Conference*, (Washington, DC, USA), pp. 81–88, IEEE Computer Society, 2004.

[32] B. B. Nasution, A. I. Khan, and E. A. Kendall, "Incorporating graph neurons (gns) to the trusted transient simple network (ttsn) security control system architecture," in *IASTED Conf. on Software Engineering*, pp. 13–19, 2005.

[33] M. Baqer, A. I. Khan, and Z. A. Baig, "Implementing a graph neuron array for pattern recognition within unstructured wireless sensor networks," in *EUC Workshops*, pp. 208–217, 2005.

[34] Z. A. Baig, M. Baqer, and A. I. Khan, "A pattern recognition scheme for distributed denial of service (ddos) attacks in wireless sensor networks," in *ICPR (3)*, pp. 1050–1054, 2006.

[35] F. Song, H. Liu, D. Zhang, and J. Yang, "A highly scalable incremental facial feature extraction method," *Neurocomputing*, vol. 71, no. 10-12, pp. 1883–1888, 2008. Neurocomputing for Vision Research; Advances in Blind Signal Processing.

[36] M. Mavroforakis and S. Theodoridis, "A geometric approach to support vector machine (svm) classification," *Neural Networks, IEEE Transactions on*, vol. 17, pp. 671–682, May 2006.

[37] L. Fei-Fei, R. Fergus, and P. Perona, "One-shot learning of object cate-gories," *Pattern Analysis and Machine Intelligence, IEEE Transactions on*, vol. 28, pp. 594–611, April 2006.

[38] E. Miller, N. Matsakis, and P. Viola, "Learning from one example through shared densities on transforms," in *Computer Vision and Pattern Recognition, 2000. Proceedings. IEEE Conference on*, vol. 1, pp. 464–471, 2000.

[39] S. K. Foo, P. Saratchandran, and N. Sundararajan, "Comparison of parallel and serial implementation of feedforward neural networks," *J. Microcomput. Appl.*, vol. 18, no. 1, pp. 83–94, 1995.

[40] N. Ikeda, P. Watta, M. Artiklar, and M. H. Hassoun, "A two-level ham-ming network for high performance associative memory," *Neural Net-works*, vol. 14, no. 9, pp. 1189–1200, 2001.

[41] X. Mu, P. Watta, and M. Hassoun, "A weighted voting model of as-sociative memory," *Neural Networks, IEEE Transactions on*, vol. 18, pp. 756–777, May 2007.

[42] E. Kokiopoulou and P. Frossard, "Distributed svm applied to image classification," in *Multimedia and Expo, 2006 IEEE International Con-ference on*, pp. 1753–1756, July 2006.

[43] V. Lobo, N. Bandeira, and F. Moura-Pires, "Ship recognition using dis-tributed self organizing maps," in *Proceedings of the 1998 International Conference on Engineering Applications of Neural Networks (EANN98)*, pp. 326–329, 1998.

[44] V. Kumar, S. Shekhar, and M. B. Amin, "A scalable parallel formulation of the backpropagation algorithm for hypercubes and related architec-tures," *IEEE Trans. Parallel Distrib. Syst.*, vol. 5, no. 10, pp. 1073–1090, 1994.

[45] A. Yang, R. Jafari, P. Kuryloski, S. Iyengar, S. S. Sastry, and R. Bajcsy, "Distributed segmentation and classification of human actions using a wearable motion sensor network," tech. rep., Electrical Engineering and Computer Sciences, University of California at Berkeley, 2007. Accessed March 17, 2010.

[46] A. I. Khan and A. Muhamad Amin, "One shot associative memory method for distorted pattern recognition," in *AI 2007: Advances in Ar-tificial Intelligence*, (Berlin/Heidelberg), pp. 705–709, Springer, 2007. Accessed October 6, 2010.

[47] R. C. Wilson, E. R. Hancock, and B. Luo, "Pattern vectors from alge-braic graph theory," *IEEE Transactions on Pattern Analysis and Ma-chine Intelligence*, vol. 27, no. 7, pp. 1112–1124, 2005.

[48] S. Auwatanamongkol, "Inexact graph matching using a genetic algorithm for image recognition," *Pattern Recognition Letters*, vol. 28, no. 12, pp. 1428–1437, 2007.

[49] A. Albiol, D. Monzo, A. Martin, J. Sastre, and A. Albiol, "Face recognition using hog-ebgm," *Pattern Recognition Letters*, vol. 29, no. 10, pp. 1537–1543, 2008.

[50] T. S. Caetano, J. J. McAuley, L. Cheng, Q. V. Le, and A. J. Smola, "Learning graph matching," *IEEE Transactions on Pattern Analysis and Machine Intelligence*, vol. 31, pp. 1048–1058, 2009.

[51] M. R. Garey and D. S. Johnson, *Computers and Intractability; A Guide to the Theory of NP-Completeness*. New York, NY, USA: W. H. Freeman & Co., 1990.

[52] B. B. Nasution, *Trusted Transaction Secure Network: Agent-Based Distributed Security Control System for Traffic on the Internet*. PhD thesis, Faculty of Information Technology, Monash University, 2007.

[53] E. Bengoetxea, *Inexact Graph Matching Using Estimation of Distribution Algorithms*. PhD thesis, Département Traitement du Signal et des Images, Ecole Nationale Supérieure des Télécommunications, 2003.

[54] A. H. M. Amin and A. I. Khan, "Parallel pattern recognition using a single-cycle learning approach within wireless sensor networks," in *PDCAT: Ninth International Conference on Parallel and Distributed Computing, Applications and Technologies, PDCAT 2008*, Dunedin, Otago, New Zealand, December 1-4, 2008, pp. 305–308, 2008.

[55] A. H. Muhamad Amin and A. I. Khan, "Commodity-grid based distributed pattern recognition framework," in *AusGrid '08: Proceedings of the Sixth Australasian Workshop on Grid Computing and e-Research*, (Darlinghurst, Australia), pp. 27–34, Australian Computer Society, Inc., 2008.

[56] A. H. Basirat, A. H. M. Amin, and A. I. Khan, "Under the cloud: A novel content addressable data framework for cloud parallelization to create and virtualize new breeds of cloud applications," in *NCA*, pp. 168–173, 2010.

[57] W. Gropp, R. Thakur, and E. Lusk, *Using MPI-2: Advanced Features of the Message Passing Interface*. Cambridge, MA, USA: MIT Press, 1999.

[58] Wikipedia, "One-shot learning," 2008. [Online; Accessed January 26, 2012].

[59] B. Lake, R. Salakhutdinov, and J. Gross, "One-shot learning of simple visual concepts," in *Proceedings of the 33rd Annual Conference of the Cognitive Science Society*, 2011.

[60] E. Bart and S. Ullman, "Cross-generalization: learning novel classes from a single example by feature replacement," in *Proceedings of the 2005 IEEE Computer Society Conference on Computer Vision and Pattern Recognition (CVPR 05)*, IEEE Press, 2005.

[61] A. I. Khan, A. H. Muhamad Amin, and R. Raja Mahmood, "Lightweight event detection scheme using distributed hierarchical graph neuron in wireless sensor networks," in *Wireless Sensor Networks*, In-Tech Publications, 2010. In-Press.

[62] M. Baqer and A. Khan, "Energy-efficient pattern recognition approach for wireless sensor networks," in *Intelligent Sensors, Sensor Networks and Information, 2007. ISSNIP 2007. 3rd International Conference on*, pp. 509–514, December 2007.

[63] A. Muhamad Amin and A. I. Khan, "Collaborative-comparison learning for complex event detection using distributed hierarchical graph neuron (dhgn) approach in wireless sensor network," in *AI 2009: Advances in Artificial Intelligence*, (Berlin/Heidelberg), pp. 111–120, Springer, 2009. Accessed October 6, 2010.

[64] A. I. Khan, A. H. Muhamad Amin, and R. A. Raja Mahmood, "An on-line scheme for threat detection within mobile ad hoc networks," in *Research in Mobile Intelligence*, John Wiley & Sons, Inc., 2010.

[65] I. Román-Godínez, I. López-Yáñez, and C. Yáñez-Márquez, "Classifying patterns in bioinformatics databases by using alpha-beta associative memories," *Biomedical Data and Applications*, pp. 187–210, 2009.

[66] B. Kosko, "Bidirectional associative memories," *IEEE Trans. Syst. Man Cybern.*, vol. 18, no. 1, pp. 49–60, 1988.

[67] B. Kosko, *Neural Networks and Fuzzy Systems: A Dynamical Systems Approach to Machine Intelligence*. Upper Saddle River, NJ, USA: Prentice-Hall, Inc., 1992.

[68] G. Ritter, P. Sussner, and J. Diaz-de Leon, "Morphological associative memories," *Neural Networks, IEEE Transactions on*, vol. 9, pp. 281–293, March 1998.

[69] R. Battiti and A. M. Colla, "Democracy in neural nets: voting schemes for classification," *Neural Netw.*, vol. 7, no. 4, pp. 691–707, 1994.

[70] L. I. Kuncheva, *Combining Pattern Classifiers: Methods and Algorithms*. Wiley-Interscience, 2004.

[71] B. Cruz, H. Sossa, and R. Barrón, "A new two-level associative memory for efficient pattern restoration," *Neural Process. Lett.*, vol. 25, no. 1, pp. 1–16, 2007.

[72] V. Chitkara, M. A. Nascimento, and C. Mastaller, "Content-based image retrieval using binary signatures," Tech. Rep. 00-18, University of Alberta, 2001.

[73] A. H. Muhamad Amin, R. A. Raja Mahmood, and A. I. Khan, "Analysis of pattern recognition algorithms using associative memory approach: A comparative study between the hopfield network and distributed hierarchical graph neuron (DHGN)," in *CITWORKSHOPS '08: Proceedings of the 2008 IEEE 8th International Conference on Computer and Information Technology Workshops*, (Washington, DC, USA), pp. 153–158, IEEE Computer Society, 2008.

[74] G. von Laszewski, I. T. Foster, and J. Gawor, "Cog kits: a bridge between commodity distributed computing and high-performance grids," in *Java Grande*, pp. 97–106, 2000.

[75] G. von Laszewski and M. Hategan, "Workflow concepts of the java cog kit," *J. Grid Comput.*, vol. 3, no. 3-4, pp. 239–258, 2005.

[76] I. Foster, Y. Zhao, I. Raicu, and S. Lu, "Cloud Computing and Grid Computing 360-Degree Compared," in *2008 Grid Computing Environments Workshop*, pp. 1–10, IEEE, November 2008.

[77] O. D. Sahin, F. Emekci, D. Agrawal, and A. E. Abbadi, "Content-based similarity search over peer-to-peer systems," in *In Proceedings of DBISP2P04*, pp. 61–78, 2004.

[78] D. S. Milojicic, V. Kalogeraki, R. Lukose, K. Nagaraja, J. Pruyne, B. Richard, S. Rollins, and Z. Xu, "Peer-to-peer computing," tech. rep., 2003.

[79] H. ku Lee, B. Carpenter, G. Fox, and S. B. Lim, "Hpjava: Programming support for high-performance grid-enabled applications," *International Journal of Parallel Algorithms and Applications*, vol. 19, p. 2004, 2004.

[80] NVIDIA, "What is GPU computing?," 2012.

[81] J. Fung and S. Mann, "Using multiple graphics cards as a general purpose parallel computer: Applications to computer vision," in *Proceedings of the Pattern Recognition, 17th International Conference on (ICPR'04) Vol. 1*, ICPR '04, (Washington, DC, USA), pp. 805–808, IEEE Computer Society, 2004.

[82] D. B. Kirk and W.-m. W. Hwu, *Programming Massively Parallel Processors: A Hands-on Approach*. San Francisco, CA, USA: Morgan Kaufmann Publishers Inc., 1st ed., 2010.

[83] R. Tsuchiyama, T. Nakamura, T. Iizuka, and A. Asahara, *The OpenCL Programming Book*. Fixstars Corporation, 2010.

[84] S. Nagarajan, "Data integrity and availability: The challenge of scale for modern storage systems," *Computer*, 2012.

[85] S. Theodoridis and K. Koutroumbas, *Pattern Recognition*. San Diego, CA, USA: Academic Press, 2003.

[86] S.-T. Bow, *Pattern Recognition and Image Preprocessing*. New York, NY, USA: Marcel Dekker, Inc., 2002.

[87] S. Hongtao, D. D. Feng, and Z. Rong-chun, "Face recognition using multi-feature and radial basis function network," in *VIP '02: Selected Papers from the 2002 Pan-Sydney Workshop on Visualisation*, (Darlinghurst, Australia, Australia), pp. 51–57, Australian Computer Society, Inc., 2002.

[88] R. P. W. Duin and D. M. J. Tax, "Experiments with classifier combining rules," in *MCS '00: Proceedings of the First International Workshop on Multiple Classifier Systems*, (London, UK), pp. 16–29, Springer-Verlag, 2000.

[89] Y. Lecun, L. Bottou, Y. Bengio, and P. Haffner, "Gradient-based learning applied to document recognition," *Proceedings of the IEEE*, vol. 86, pp. 2278 –2324, November 1998.

[90] A. Frank and A. Asuncion, "UCI machine learning repository," 2010. Accessed October 6, 2010.

[91] G. von Laszewski, M. Hategan, and D. Kodeboyina, "Work coordination for grid computing," in *Grid Technologies*, Southampton, UK: WIT Press, 2006.

[92] A. H. Muhamad Amin and A. I. Khan, "Distributed multi-feature recognition scheme for greyscale images," *Neural Process. Lett.*, vol. 33, no. 1, pp. 45–59, 2011.

[93] M. A. Nascimento and V. Chitkara, "Color-based image retrieval using binary signatures," in *SAC '02: Proceedings of the 2002 ACM Symposium on Applied Computing*, (New York, NY, USA), pp. 687–692, ACM, 2002.

[94] R. Kimmel, D. Shaked, M. Elad, and I. Sobel, "Space-dependent color gamut mapping: a variational approach," *IEEE Transactions on Image Processing*, vol. 14, no. 6, pp. 796–803, 2005.

[95] R. Lämmel, "Google's mapreduce programming model; revisited," *Sci. Comput. Program.*, vol. 68, no. 3, pp. 208–237, October 2007.

[96] A. H. Muhamad Amin and A. I. Khan, "Spatio-temporal forest fire detection using a distributed hierarchical graph neuron within an integrated wireless sensor network-grid environment," in *Proceedings of the Second International Conference on Parallel, Distributed, Grid and*

Cloud Computing for Engineering, PARENG '11, (Stirlingshire, UK), Civil-Comp Press, 2011, doi: 10.4203/ccp.95.50.

[97] P. Cortez and A. Morais, "Data mining approach to predict forest fires using meteorological data," in *New Trends in Artificial Intelligence, Proceedings of the 13th EPIA 2007: Portuguese Conference on Artificial Intelligence*, pp. 512–523, 2007.

[98] A. I. Khan and A. H. Muhamad Amin, *Integrating Sensory Data within a Structural Analysis Grid*, pp. 389–412. Stirlingshire, UK: Saxe-Coburg Publications, 2009, doi:10.4203/csets.21.18.

[99] W. Sibai, *Adaptive Mesh Refinement with the Morley Thin Plate Element: Static and Free Vibration Analysis.* University College of Swansea, 1989.

[100] P. Jimack and S. Nadeem, "A parallel domain decomposition algorithm for the adaptive finite element solution of 3-D convection-diffusion problems," in *Computational Science, International Conf. on, ICCS 2002*, Springer Berlin / Heidelberg, 2002.

[101] Y. Fragakis and E. Onate, "Parallel delaunay triangulation for particle finite element methods," *Communications in Numerical Methods in Engineering*, vol. 24, no. 11, pp. 1009–1017, 2008.

[102] M. W. Maier, "Architecting principles for systems-of-systems," *Systems Engineering*, vol. 1, no. 4, pp. 267–284, 1998.

[103] H. McGurk and J. MacDonald, "Hearing lips and seeing voices," *Nature*, vol. 264, pp. 746–748, December 1976.

Index